EXPLORING CULTURES THROUGH ART

Chína and Japan

BY DIANA GRANA

SCHOLASTIC
PROFESSIONAL BOOKS

New York • Toronto • London • Auckland • Sydney
Mexico City • New Delhi • Hong Kong • Buenos Aires

FOR STANA AND ROB, AND TO THE MEMORY OF MY FATHER AND MOTHER.

ACKNOWLEDGMENTS

Teaching is always a process of collaboration. In creating the activities collected in this volume, I have benefited from the ideas of colleagues, student teachers, and my own students. For this particular volume, I would like to thank Bank Street School for Children colleagues Stanlee Brimberg, Roberta Quinn, Edith Gwathmey, and Roberta Altman, and former student teachers Lauren Berkeley, Alison Thomas, and Scott Segal. In addition, I'd like to express my appreciation to all of my students for their wonderful creativity and candid feedback.

Cover design by Josué Castilleja
Cover art by Josué Castilleja and Sarah Longhi
Interior design by Melinda Belter
Interior illustrations by Jane Dippold and Teresa Anderko
Maps by Jim McMahon

ISBN 0-439-11106-4

Contents

Using Projects and Activities in the Classroom

It is not uncommon today to hear parents and teachers alike discussing the need for students to get back to basics. More homework, a longer school day, and an extended school year are just a few of the suggestions for raising the educational standards of our children. This is a book of activities that you can do with your students as they return to basics. These projects are not a respite from learning; they *are* learning. They are intended for all students, not just those who struggle with the regular work.

As a teacher, you know that hands-on activities and projects are an important part of learning—by reinforcing what children have studied in the abstract while providing an important creative outlet. For many students, hands-on activities are an essential step in mastering content. The skills and concepts required to do such projects reflect alternate ways of demonstrating knowledge. And students who are adept at verbal and written narration find satisfaction in other forms of expression—they take pleasure in translating what they have learned into something that can be appreciated and admired.

Hands-on activities require certain very important skills. Students not only need to listen to or read instructions and follow a set procedure but they also learn to care for particular materials, be patient and orderly when it is necessary to take turns at a certain tool or piece of equipment, budget time, allocate tasks, and decide priorities. Some projects may require more than a day to finish. In such cases, students will need to remember what they have done, what they planned to do, and how to organize their work over a longer period. Often they will need to work together cooperatively to complete the activity. They may need to compromise with others or adjust their own ideas and goals. As each project is finished, it is interesting to watch students discover previously unknown strengths in themselves and their classmates. Well-planned projects and activities result not only in academic gains but also in heightened student enthusiasm, problem-solving ability, and interpersonal skills.

Projects are a means to an end. The context in which you do an individual project is extremely important. Therefore, a suggested context is provided for each one. The projects included here assume a certain amount of knowledge on the part of your students—knowledge that they have gained through a combination of reading, studying, and listening in class. Each activity is also an excellent means of assessment. Be alert to misconceptions that might be revealed in the course of doing a project. Often, what students do not understand is much more apparent when they are required to create something based on that understanding, because they cannot simply mimic what they have heard or read.

You might ask yourself these questions before planning a particular activity for the class:

What do I want students to learn from this activity? How does it increase their understanding of the topic?

Is this the best time to reinforce or enrich what students have been studying? Do they have the knowledge base to get the most out of this activity?

Can students do this activity safely? Do they have the skills, self-discipline, and maturity to handle materials in a safe and productive way?

Can the prospect of doing this activity motivate them to follow the set guidelines?

Once you have decided that a particular activity is appropriate, do the following:

- Always run through the activity yourself before trying it out with students. You may need to repeat the project to become comfortable with the materials, procedures, and timing. The finished product will serve as an excellent model for the class. Students enjoy seeing what it is they're making.

- See how long it takes *you* to do a particular activity. If it's not easy for you, it will be even more challenging for your students. They will require at least as much time as you do to complete a project. Remember to allow time for explanations, demonstrations, and the allocation of materials.

- As you calculate the time needed to complete a project, plan so that the steps in completing an activity coincide with the blocks of time you have with your students. If you have to make a judgement call, it's better to plan on accomplishing less rather than more in any particular time slot.

- If a project needs more than one day to complete, prepare a place to store the materials in the interim. If unfinished projects need to dry, flat surfaces work well. An alternative is to clip projects on paper onto a "clothesline" made of utility wire. Be sure that students can identify their work.

- Assemble all needed materials before starting. After you have done the activity yourself, verify the amounts needed of each item. Allow for mistakes—have extra materials on hand.

- List all the steps involved in completing the project.

- Set materials out in a logical way. Plan how students will obtain the items they need.

- Plan ahead how to divide up the class for working on the activity or project.

- Decide how you will assess the projects when they are completed. If you are going to assign a letter or numerical grade, what will be the criteria? Be sure to explain fully to your students how you are going to evaluate their work.

- In addition to the quality of work produced, evaluations often consider how well students worked together. Was the work shared equitably? Did students listen to the ideas of other group members? How were students' strengths or weaknesses managed? Could every group member explain what was done and why?

- Always complete an activity or project that you have started. You demonstrate responsibility to commitments when you do so. There are a few circumstances, however, when you might need to abort a project. For example, there might be some unexpected and unavoidable time difficulty, or you might conclude either that it is too difficult for your students or that they can't do the work safely. In such cases, find a way to bring the project to a logical completion point before the end, and explain fully to the class the reasons behind this change of plans.

Debriefing is an important part of doing an activity. In addition to bringing the project to closure, it helps students understand how the activity either clarifies or extends what they already know. Follow-up activities that build on projects by opening up new levels of learning (and making connections with other subjects and skills) are included for most of the projects in this book.

After projects are completed, students usually want to share what they have created. When only one group has done an activity, or when the results vary, an oral presentation might be appropriate. When the entire class has done the same project, a bulletin board or museum-type display might be the best vehicle for sharing. However, when displaying the finished projects, be sure to include every student's work. Each class member, no matter how talented, will look for his or her own project on display. Displaying everyone's work makes a statement about the value of each child in your class.

China and Japan

For over 150 years, American attitudes toward East Asia have fluctuated widely. During that time, both China and Japan have been considered exotic, isolated, and backward nations, or conversely, military and economic threats. However, one thing remains constant: Americans generally are unaware of all but the most superficial aspects of Chinese and Japanese cultures.

Although many schools now include units on China and/or Japan, most students come away from such encounters with little feel for the richness of these ancient cultures. Memorizing Chinese dynasties or reading about the Japanese attack on Pearl Harbor will not generate a sustained interest. However, when students are given an opportunity to experience a culture through activities and projects, their appreciation and understanding are immeasurably enhanced. And in our ever-shrinking world, we can no longer afford ignorance. It is important for students today to have a deeper understanding of how people live and work on the other side of the globe.

Using This Book

All the activities in this book have been classroom tested. In addition, each one specifies whether it is especially suitable for a study of China, Japan, or both. In many cases, where the project is suitable for either, one of the countries illustrates the activity. To use it for the other, you will need to make a few obvious adaptations.

The context is provided first—its length dependent on whether the subject is commonly found in textbooks. A materials list and the directions follow. Suggestions and tips derived from classroom experience are also included. When possible, try a follow-up activity to expand, enrich, and connect with other subjects. In some cases, where teachers may have difficulty locating the information (as in Chinese Names and Geography), the answers are provided.

Passports and Visas

CHINA OR JAPAN

CONTEXT

This activity will acquaint students with the function of a passport and help them create their own "official" document. Remember to prepare the cover and information pages before you begin your study of China or Japan.

DIRECTIONS

1. Create a template for an "information page." Include space for students to fill in their full name, sex, birthplace, birth date, and nationality, as well as the dates of issue and expiration.

2. Show students either an actual United States passport or a picture of one (see above) to use as a model.

3. Give each student a sheet of blue construction paper. Have them fold it in half across the width and turn the paper so that it opens like a book.

4. Each student needs to make a passport cover on the front of the construction paper. Another option is to create covers on a separate sheet of paper, cut out the words and seal, and glue them in the proper place on the construction paper.

5. Instruct students to bring from home a two-inch square picture of themselves. If students don't have a photograph, they can draw a self-portrait or you can snap a picture of them in school.

6. Ask students to fill in their information page. Remind them to sign their name at the bottom.

7. Students paste their picture in the appropriate space and insert the completed information page between the covers.

8. Finally, create several pages for "visas." These pages can be either stapled together with the cover, or attached, with removable fasteners, so they can be added as necessary.

FOLLOW-UP

I. *Visa pages are used to show work completed during your class study. These might include maps as well as drawings of modern and traditional clothing, types of housing, currency, and important sites and cities. Other pages might include a list of common occupations, recipes for typical dishes, or descriptions of holidays.*

II. *Display completed passports.*

SETTING UP

MATERIALS

✛ U.S. passport, or picture of the seal of the United States

✛ dark blue construction paper, one sheet per student

✛ gold ink or markers

✛ template of a passport information page, one copy per student

✛ picture of each student

✛ white paper cut in half

TEACHING TIPS

If the class is just beginning to study a foreign land, be sure they understand the definition of *country* or *nation*.

■

Have students discuss the function of a passport as well as the procedure for obtaining one.

■

In order to "travel" to another country to learn about its land, people, and customs, each student will need the newly-created passport.

■

Chinese Names and Geography
CHINA

CONTEXT

When students start learning about China, they are often intimidated by the prospect of learning a long list of complicated Chinese names. You can help them overcome their fears by first doing pronunciation exercises together, and then giving them a fun puzzle to solve. This activity helps demystify Chinese names and students will enjoy it.

This geography exercise focuses on Chinese place names. Have a large map of China handy so students can see the correlation between each name and its geographic location. Or distribute a copy of reproducible page 14 to each student. The names of major provinces, rivers, islands, seas, and cities are all shown there.

Note: Approximate pronunciation is provided using the *pinyin* system, the standard spelling for Chinese names on most modern maps, atlases, and books. Practice yourself until you feel comfortable.

SOUNDS PRONUNCIATION

Vowels

a=ah   Han (Hahn), Tang (Tahng), Shang (Shahng)
e=uh   Deng (Duhng)
i=ee   Jin (Jeen)
o=oo (as in look)   Song (Soong)
u=oo (as in food)   Chu (Choo)
i after c, s, or z=uh   Sichuan (Suh-chwan), Yangzi (Yahng-dzuh)
i after ch, sh, or zh=ur   chifan (chur-fahn), Shikai (Shur-kai), Zhili (Jur-lee)

Compound vowels

ao=ow/au   Mao (Mau)
yi=ee   Yibin (Ee-been)
iu=yo   Liu (Lyo)
ou=oh   Ouyang (Oh-yahng)

Consonants The same as English EXCEPT:

c=ts   Cixi (Tsuh-syi)
q=ch   Qin (Cheen)
x=sh   Xiaoping (Shyau-peeng)
z=dz   Zedong (Dzuh-doong)
zh=j   Zhou (Joe)

CHINESE GEOGRAPHY WORDS

Geographic Features	Directions and Location	Colors	Miscellaneous Words	Numbers
shan - mountain(s)		huang - yellow	jing - capital	yi - 1
he - river	dong - east	qing - blue	yun - cloud(s)	er - 2
shaan - mountain pass	nan - south	hei - black	long - dragon	san - 3
jiang - river	xi - west		chang - long	si - 4
tai - terrace	bei - north			wu - 5
chuan - river	shang - on			liu - 6
hu - lake				qi - 7
hai - sea				ba - 8
wan - bay				jiu - 9
				shi - 10

DIRECTIONS

1. Distribute the list of Chinese geography words.

2. After going over the list with the class, ask students to look at a map of China.

3. See how many of the words students can combine to form the names of Chinese provinces, cities, islands, rivers, and seas.

4. Have students write down, translate, and locate as many names as they can.

MATERIALS

✛ list of Chinese geography words and their meanings (page 8)

✛ map of China showing the names of provinces, rivers, islands, seas, and cities; *China* map (page 14)

Answer Key

1. Shandong (east of the mountains) - province
2. Shanxi (west of the mountains) - province
3. Hubei (north of the lake) - province
4. Hunan (south of the lake) - province
5. Hebei (north of the river) - province
6. Henan (south of the river) - province
7. Qinghai (blue lake) - province
8. Sichuan (4 rivers) - province
9. Shaanxi (west of the pass) - province
10. Jiangxi (west of the river) - province
11. Yunnan (south of the clouds) - province
12. Taiwan (terrace bay) - island
13. Hainan (sea [to the] south) - island
14. Beijing (northern capital) - city
15. Nanjing (southern capital) - city
16. Shanghai (on the sea) - city
17. Xi Jiang (West River) - river
18. Heilong Jiang (Black Dragon River) - river
19. Huang He (Yellow River) - river
20. Chang Jiang (Long [Yangtze] River) - river

TEACHING TIPS

Provide spaces for your students to write about 20 names at the bottom of the list. This is usually enough to keep even the most eager students engaged, although not all children will be able to fill the page.

■

Sometimes students turn words around in translating them. Urge them to find the place on the map before deciding how to translate the name. The translations provided make the most sense given the location.

■

FOLLOW-UP

I. *Keep the list on page 8 handy for future reference. For example, point out that Mao Zedong came from Hunan province and that Beijing is the present capital of China.*
II. *Encourage students to find examples of place names in other countries that relate to location.*

Exploring the Coast

CHINA OR JAPAN

CONTEXT

Before beginning this activity, ask students to study or review a variety of different coastal land and water forms. By using the map of China on reproducible page 14, this exercise helps students learn about some of the geographic features of China's long 11,185-mile coastline. You can use the same types of questions to study Japan.

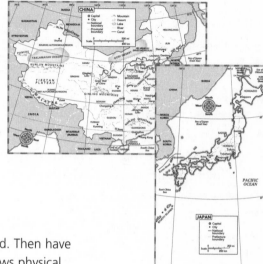

DIRECTIONS

1. Instruct students to work with a partner. Have them take turns locating and writing down the answers.

2. Before they begin, tell students to look at the key or legend. Then have them refer to the map of China and decide whether it shows physical or political features.

3. Ask several preview questions to give the class a quick overview of East Asia. Have them answer in geographic terms or names; you can use a fill-in-the-blank format. Below are some sample statements (the answers are in boldface).

- China is located on the **mainland** of Asia.

- North and South Korea together share a **peninsula**.

- The **Sea of Japan** separates Japan from Russia and Korea.

- Japan is an **archipelago**.

- The **Korean Strait** separates Korea and Japan.

- To the east of Asia lies the **Pacific** Ocean.

MATERIALS

+ Rand McNally's *Quick Reference World Atlas* (the most detailed map of China in a classroom atlas), one China (or Japan) map for every two students (page 14)

+ list of sample questions with space to fill in the answers (page 11)

+ pencils

4. Students can begin exploring the coast of China by "boat." Have them start at the southern border and sail north, staying as close to the coast as possible. As they travel have them answer questions like the following (the answers are in boldface):

- What body of water are you starting from? **Gulf of Tonkin**

- What country, other than China, borders this body of water? **Vietnam**

- As you travel north, you will pass three important Chinese islands. List them: **Hainan, Hong Kong (Xianggang), Taiwan** (Hint: The first one is near the middle of the page, the second has recently been returned to China, and the third has a different Chinese government.)

- What three seas do you sail through? List them in order from south to north. **South China Sea, East China Sea, Yellow Sea**

- There is actually a fourth "sea," but its name is given only in Chinese. The Chinese word for "sea" is *hai*. Write the name of this sea. **Bo Hai**

- There are three important peninsulas on the Chinese coast. The most southern one is called *Leizhou Peninsula*.
  Where is it located? **Between the Gulf of Tonkin and the South China Sea** or **north of Hainan Island**

- Find the other two peninsulas. The one to the north is called the *Liaodong* peninsula. Write the name of the large city near the tip of this peninsula. **Dalian** The peninsula to the south is called the *Shandong* peninsula. What is the large city on the southern coast of this peninsula? **Qingdao** What body of water do these two peninsulas enclose? **Bo Hai**

- There are several straits along the coast of China. On your map, however, only one is given a name. What is that strait called? **Taiwan Strait**

- What is the large port city nearest the capital? **Tianjin**

- Use a ruler and the map scale to tell how far *in miles* the capital of China is from the sea. **85 miles**

- On what type of geographic feature is the city of Hangzhou located? **Bay**

- Shanghai is located at the mouth of what river? **Yangtze** (also called **Chang Jiang**)

- What Chinese city on or near the coast borders North Korea? **Dandong**

- What river forms the border between China and North Korea? **Yalu River**

- What body of water do China, North Korea, and South Korea all border? **Yellow Sea**

Elevation Map
CHINA OR JAPAN

CONTEXT

By having students create their own elevation map, this activity not only reinforces the geography of China or Japan but also familiarizes students with the most commonly used map symbols. In addition, it provides the basis for future research, art, and writing projects.

Before beginning this activity, have students review the definition of an elevation map.

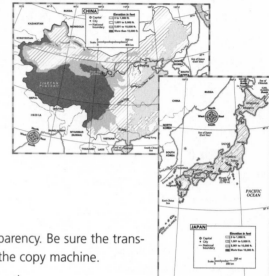

DIRECTIONS

1. Use the elevation map to create a photocopy on the transparency. Be sure the transparency is safe for photocopying; otherwise it will melt in the copy machine.

2. Now examine the paper elevation map with students. Be sure they understand what it shows. Discuss the various ways to indicate elevation on black and white maps, as well as on colored maps. If you are using a black and white map, you might want to have students color in the key and then fill in the map accordingly.

3. Attach mural paper to the wall in a place in the classroom or hallway where students can work over a period of days without having to remove the paper from the wall. Be sure to mark with masking tape the place on the floor where the projector is.

4. Set up the overhead projector and map transparency. Center the projection of the map on the mural paper. Either tape the transparency to the glass of the overhead projector, or mark the place carefully so that the transparency can be put in the same place when returning to the project.

5. Divide the class into several groups, one for each of the following tasks: outlining the map onto the mural paper, coloring the map, creating a map key, and adding a compass rose and appropriate title.

6. With the transparency as their guide, the first group of students can outline the boundaries of the country onto the mural paper.

7. The second group can then paint the appropriate landmasses green and the bodies of water blue.

8. When the map is completely dry, another group of students can pencil in any areas of higher elevation and paint them yellow.

9. Pencil in and paint each successive rising level of elevation. If you are making a map of China, surrounding countries should be painted a neutral color. Indicate borders with a marker, if you wish.

MATERIALS

+ transparency safe for photocopy machine use
+ elevation map of China or Japan (page 15)
+ overhead projector
+ masking tape
+ large sheet of brown or white mural paper
+ pencils
+ blue, green, yellow, and brown paints
+ black markers

10. When all painted surfaces have dried, another group of students can add the map key showing elevations at one corner of the paper. You might want to have them leave room for additional information.

11. Have the final group come up with an appropriate title and design a directional arrow or compass rose.

FOLLOW-UP

I. Art *While some students are creating the elevation map, the rest of the class can browse through books, magazines, or postcards that depict the country you are studying. Each student should select a picture they find appealing.*

1. Have students draw the picture they have chosen on one of the blank index cards. Some students like to depict the scene as accurately as possible; others prefer a much more impressionistic rendition. After they have finished drawing, students should label their card and write their name on the back.

2. Help students locate and label their particular site on the painted elevation map. If more than one student has portrayed a spot, they can work as a group to identify the correct location.

3. Staple one end of a piece of yarn or string to each index card. Attach the other end to the map, as close to the site depicted on the card as possible. Try to obscure the map's information as little as possible. If there are a number of cards for the same site, twist them together and staple all the yarn leads onto the map.

4. Finally, allow time for students to view the map and discuss the places they have chosen.

II. Research *Have students do mini research projects on the sites they have chosen, which they can present either in written form or orally. Remind students to refer to the elevation map as well as to their picture card.*

III. Literature and Writing *Since Japanese and Chinese poetry often uses language to create a vivid image of our surroundings, try doing a literature unit on poetry at the same time that your students study geography.*

Then do the following activity: Ask students to select a favorite poem (one they have read at home or in class). Instruct them to copy and illustrate the work. You can also encourage them to create their own poetry using as much natural imagery as possible. The completed poems can be displayed around the elevation map along with the picture cards.

MATERIALS

✛ pictures of places in the country

✛ 4- by 6-inch blank index cards

✛ colored pencils, paints, and/or markers

✛ yarn or string

✛ stapler

✛ political map of East Asia; China or Japan map (page 14)

TEACHING TIPS

Make your own simplified elevation map using the map of China on page 15. Outline the different levels in pencil, then use several colors or black and white indicators (such as stripes) to show differences in elevation. Trace everything in black pen for better copying.

■

Groups of two to five students usually work best. Not every task requires the same number of students. In general, the number of students needed decreases with each step. Because tasks must be done consecutively, the rest of the class will need other work to do while individual groups work on their tasks.

■

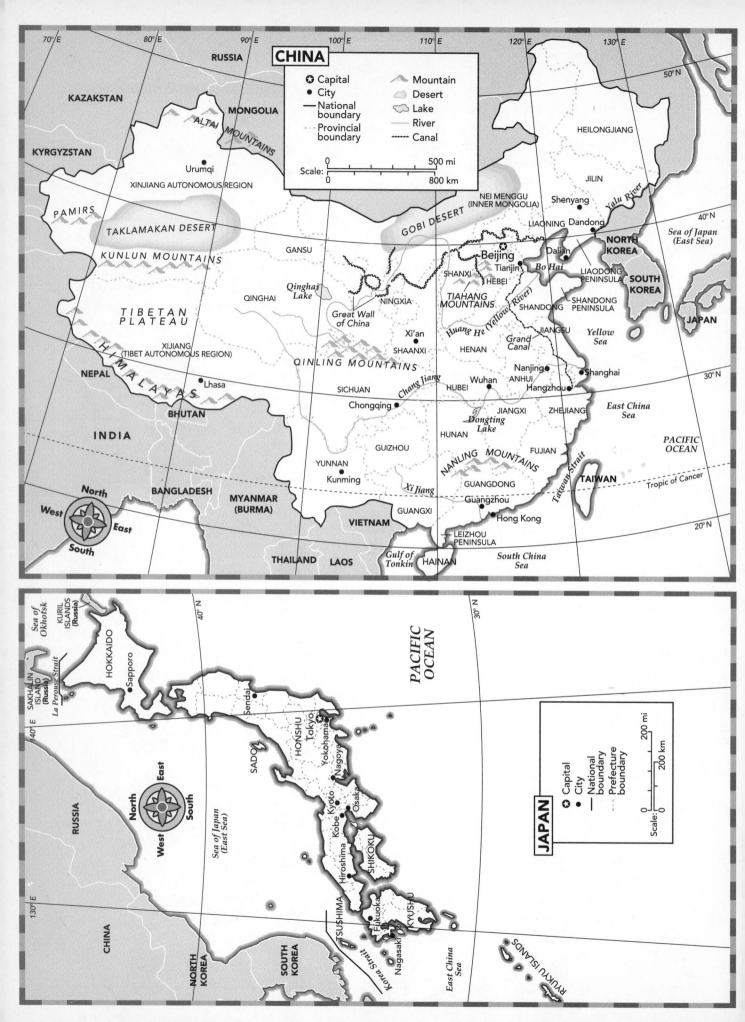

Scholastic Professional Books Exploring Cultures Through Art: China and Japan

CHINA

Elevation in feet
- ☆ Capital
- ● City
- — National boundary

Elevation in feet	
	0 to 1,000 ft.
	1,001 to 5,000 ft.
	5,001 to 10,000 ft.
	More than 10,000 ft.

Scale:
0 — 500 mi
0 — 800 km

RUSSIA

KAZAKSTAN

MONGOLIA

KYRGYZSTAN

NORTH KOREA

Beijing

Bo Hai

SOUTH KOREA

Great Wall of China

JAPAN

TIBETAN PLATEAU

Huang He (Yellow River)

Yellow Sea

NEPAL

Chang Jiang

Shanghai

BHUTAN

East China Sea

INDIA

PACIFIC OCEAN

North
West East
South

BANGLADESH

MYANMAR (BURMA)

Xi Jiang

TAIWAN

Tropic of Cancer

VIETNAM

Hong Kong

Taiwan Strait

20° N

THAILAND LAOS

Gulf of Tonkin

HAINAN

South China Sea

70° E 80° E 90° E 100° E 110° E 120° E 130° E
50° N 40° N 30° N

JAPAN

Elevation in feet
	0 to 1,000 ft.
	1,001 to 5,000 ft.
	5,001 to 10,000 ft.
	More than 10,000 ft.

200 mi
200 km
Scale:
0 — 0

- ☆ Capital
- ● City
- — National boundary

Sea of Okhotsk

KURIL ISLANDS (Russia)

SAKHALIN ISLAND (Russia)

La Perouse Strait

HOKKAIDO

Sapporo

PACIFIC OCEAN

SADO

Sendai

HONSHU

Tokyo

Mount Fuji 12,388 ft. (3,776 m)

North
West East
South

RUSSIA

Sea of Japan (East Sea)

Kyoto

Osaka

SHIKOKU

CHINA

Hiroshima

TSUSHIMA

Korea Strait

NORTH KOREA

SOUTH KOREA

Nagasaki

KYUSHU

East China Sea

RYUKYU ISLANDS

140° E 130° E
40° N 30° N

16

Fans

CHINA OR JAPAN

CONTEXT

Fans have been cooling off the people of China and Japan for thousands of years. Although air conditioning and electric fans have made hand-operated fans obsolete, they are still an important part of Asian culture. Even today, traditional dances, formal attire, and dramatic performances often require the use of elegantly decorated fans.

There are two basic kinds of fans: the folding fan and the flat, or rigid, fan. The folding fan can be constructed either from separate pieces of paper joined together or from one single sheet of paper. All types of fans lend themselves to beautiful decoration and are works of art in themselves.

Folding Fan

DIRECTIONS 1 (easy version)

1. Turn the Manila drawing paper so that it is wider than it is long. Decorate the top half. The bottom half will become the handle. If you use paint, allow it to dry before handling. Decorate the back, if you wish.

2. Start at one side and fold the paper in accordion pleats. The pleats should run vertically.

3. Pull the bottom of the pleats together (the undecorated half) and fasten with masking tape. Color the tape to make an attractive handle.

4. Spread the fan open to use. Note: This makes a narrow, but sturdy, V-shaped fan.

DIRECTIONS 2 (challenging version)

BEFORE YOU BEGIN

To create a template for students to copy on plain or scrap paper, draw a pair of parallel curves, one above the other, for the top and bottom of the fan. The top curve should be longer than the bottom curve. The resulting shape should also be wider horizontally than vertically. The distance between the top and bottom curves must be uniform. Connect the left end of the top curve with the left end of the bottom curve by drawing a straight line between them. Repeat on the right side of the curves to close the shape, and cut out the template. Have students do the following:

1. Draw the outline of the fan-shaped template on a piece of Manila paper.

CULTURE

MATERIALS 1

✛ Manila drawing paper

✛ paint (tempura or water-color), markers, or crayons

✛ scissors

✛ masking tape

MATERIALS 2

✛ template for fan-shaped outline

✛ Manila drawing paper

✛ pencils

✛ paint (tempura or watercolor), markers, or crayons

✛ cardboard sticks or strips

✛ glue

✛ scissors

✛ masking tape

2. Decorate the fan before you cut it out. If you use paint, allow it to dry before handling.

3. Cut out the fan shape. Decorate the other side, if you wish (part of the back will be covered by sticks).

4. Fold the paper in accordion pleats, slightly wider on the top than on the bottom. Keep the bottom of the pleats together.

5. Cut thin cardboard strips about 7 inches long that will fit in the folded sections. (Cut one strip for every other fold.)

6. Temporarily tape one end of the cardboard stick to each of the folds to test the length and position. Be sure you have one stick for the last fold on either end. Allow an inch or so of each stick to overlap the fan paper. Then glue the sticks to the back of the fan. Line the sticks up so that they lie one on top of the other when the fan is folded.

7. Using masking tape, fasten the free end of the sticks together and decorate the handle.

Flat Fan

DIRECTIONS

1. Draw the outline of two identical shapes (circle, oval, square, or rectangle) on stiff paper to create the two sides of the fan. If you make a square or rectangle, round off the corners. If you draw a circle, use a compass or large circular object.

2. Decorate the fan shapes on the front and back before cutting them out. If you use paint, allow it to dry before handling.

3. Cut out the fan shapes.

4. Glue together three pairs of craft sticks end to end, with a two-inch overlap.

5. Glue each of the three long sticks to the back of the front panel of the fan, with the bottom ends coming together. If you need more support at the corners, add two additional ribs.

6. Make a handle using two sets of three to five craft sticks, depending on the number of ribs. Tape each set together at the top and bottom.

7. Tape the ribs to the top of one set, so the masking tape is on the inside. Cover the first set with the second, again with the tape on the inside.

8. Now glue the back of the fan to the ribs.

9. Wrap masking tape around the handle, and color or paint to match the rest of the fan.

FOLLOW-UP

I. *Use your collection of handmade fans as accessories in class performances of Asian drama. (See* Bunraku Puppets, *page 54, and* Noh Mask, *page 36.)*

TEACHING TIPS

To make sticks or strips to use with the folding fan, use the kind of cardboard that is shiny on one side (such as shirt box cardboard). It will support the fan, but it is also thin and somewhat flexible. The bottoms of the strips will come together and bend just enough to make a handle.

■

Creating the template for the flat fan shape is tricky. Use a compass or large circular object to make the top curve. The fan should be at least four inches from top to bottom.

■

MATERIALS

+ stiff paper
+ pencils
+ compass (optional)
+ paints (tempura or watercolor), markers, or crayons
+ craft sticks
+ glue
+ scissors
+ masking tape

Handmade Paper

CHINA OR JAPAN

CONTEXT

Paper was invented in China in the second century B.C. The oldest piece of paper ever found dates back to that century. The oldest sheet of paper with writing on it, also discovered in China, dates back to 110 A.D. In addition to its use as a writing surface, paper was used in China for clothing, wrapping, toilet paper, kite-making, wall covering, money, umbrellas, artificial flowers, cut decorations, and a variety of other items. Knowledge of paper-making spread from China to India in the seventh century, and then onward to West Asia. It did not reach Europe until the twelfth century.

This activity can be used when students are learning about writing in either China or Japan (page 20). It allows them to see that with relatively few raw materials and simple equipment, they can make something as common as paper.

DIRECTIONS

Prepare ahead of time by soaking pieces of paper in a bowl of water overnight. (The materials and amounts listed are suitable for a group of two or three students.)

1. Fill the blender halfway with warm water. Add a handful of the soaked paper. Cover and blend at medium speed until the individual pieces are gone and the pulp has a thick consistency.

2. Pour the pulp into the basin and mix thoroughly.

3. Slide the deckle into the basin and hold it underwater. Move it gently back and forth to get an even layer of fibers.

4. Being careful to keep the deckle flat, lift it out of the water and allow to drain. There should now be an even layer of pulp on the screen.

5. Gently press on the pulp with your hand to remove the excess water. Place a sponge on the other side of the screen to absorb any remaining moisture while you press.

6. Place a clean dry towel on a flat surface and flip the deckle over onto it. The paper should gently fall onto the mat.

7. Carefully lift the deckle, making sure to leave the paper on the towel.

8. Place another towel or blotter on the top of the paper. Iron the damp paper between two pieces of towel. After the paper has dried, remove it from the towel.

MATERIALS

+ electric blender for cutting fibers into pulp
+ electric iron
+ scrap paper torn into little pieces (about 1-inch square)
+ 1 large bowl
+ deckle (wooden frame with metal screen covering one side)
+ large basin or aluminum foil roasting pan
+ dish towels/paper towels
+ sponge

FOLLOW-UP

I. Have students use brush pens and ink to write characters on their own sheets of handmade paper. Mount each character on a piece of colored construction paper and display prominently around the classroom.

II. Possible research topics:
    The spread of paper from China to the West
    Ways of making paper
    Uses of paper

III. Research or discussion topic:
    The connection between paper, printing, and the dissemination of knowledge

Calligraphy
CHINA OR JAPAN

CONTEXT

Rather than using an alphabet, Chinese writing consists of ideographs or—as they're commonly know in English—characters. Traditionally, the language was written vertically from the top of the page to the bottom, starting in the upper right-hand corner. Although the Japanese spoken language is completely different from Chinese, Japanese use Chinese characters as an integral part of their writing system. In Japanese, the ideographs are called *kanji*, which means "Chinese words." This activity can be used when studying either culture.

The practice of calligraphy helps reinforce what students have learned about written Chinese or Japanese *kanji*. It not only provides them with the experience of using traditional tools of writing, but also helps them understand the Asian attitude toward the written word. (See "Topics for Discussion" to extend this aspect of calligraphy practice.)

DIRECTIONS

1. Demonstrate how to grind ink using a traditional ink stick and ink stone. Pass the materials around so that each student gets a chance to grind the ink—students love doing this. It also becomes apparent how long it takes to get dark-colored ink this way. A Chinese or Japanese scholar, calligrapher, or painter used this meditative time to prepare for writing or painting.

2. Put a small amount of commercial ink into several small paper cups. You will need one cup for each group of two or three students. Pour a small amount of water into another cup.

3. Students should dip their brush pen first in the water, wiping it off on the edge of the cup, and then in the ink, wiping it again to remove any excess liquid.

4. Ruled or folded squares of paper about 1 1/2 inches square or larger work best. You don't have to use expensive rice paper, but construction paper is too absorbent. For practice, use 8 1/2- by 11-inch white paper folded into 8 or 16 boxes.

MATERIALS

+ chart of Chinese characters (*kanji* in Japanese) (page 23)
+ paper
+ medium-sized calligraphy brush pens, one for each student (You can purchase these from any art supplier. Don't buy the ones that are already inked.)
+ 1 ink stone and ink stick
+ 1 quart of black ink
+ small paper cups for ink and water
+ paper towels at each table to absorb excess water or ink or to mop up spills

5. Emphasize the location of the brush in the hand: the shaft remains perpendicular to the paper, held with the thumb extended and the other fingers positioned along the back. (See illustration on the next page.) There is more movement of the wrist and arm and less movement of the small muscles of the fingers than in Western writing. The strokes should be bone-like, that is, slightly broader at the ends than in the middle. This is accomplished by varying the pressure on the brush, and by doubling back over the beginning and end of each stroke.

6. Using the models provided, students should practice writing Chinese characters in the boxes.

7. Later, have each student select a particular character to write in isolation as a display. (See Follow-up.)

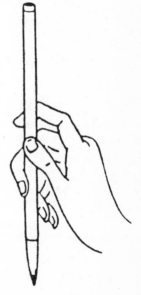

TIP

Cover desks or tabletops with newspaper and secure it with masking tape. Have students bring in old shirts to wear as smocks—the ink used for calligraphy is water soluble, but it might still stain clothing. Paper plates or sticks made from taped, rolled-up newspaper serve as good brush rests. Explain to your students that if they stand the long brushes in the short cups of ink, their cups may tilt and spill.

■

With a large, conventional paintbrush, demonstrate the order of strokes by "painting" with water on the chalkboard. In general, start from the upper left-hand corner, the top, or the outside perimeter. Sample characters (page 21) have numbers to indicate the correct order.

■

Calligraphers practice their strokes and characters thousands of times before they are taken seriously as artists. Insist on quiet for concentration, and have students repeat the same characters at least eight times before attempting new ones. Ask them to circle their best ones.

■

If you live in an area with Chinese or Japanese stores, you might want to buy a half dozen ink sticks and ink stones, one for each group of students. The brushes, ink sticks, and stones should last for years.

■

Begin cleanup ten minutes before the end of the session. Have one person from each table take the leftover ink and pour it carefully into a pitcher. Have another student collect the brushes and wash them under cold water. Warm water will loosen the glue holding the brushes in place. Because washing the brushes will make a mess, be sure that some students are assigned the job of cleaning up the sink as well.

■

Brushes should be damp-dried with paper towels and placed upright in a high, open container. Have the students who aren't washing brushes transfer finished papers to a drying place and remove all newspaper from the desktops.

■

SPECIAL FEATURES OF WRITING CHARACTERS

To grind ink, put a small amount of tap water on the ink stone. Dip one end of the stick in the water, move it to the raised area of the stone, and rub gently. The ink collects in a shallow well at one end of the stone. Repeat the process until the water is dark enough to use for writing. *Note:* Use only one end of the stick so that you can hold the other.

East Asians believe there is a proper way to write characters. It is important to sit up straight with both feet on the floor when writing with a brush pen. It allows the *qi*, or energy, to flow through the body to the hand of the calligrapher. Once the stroke is begun, it is completed and left alone—no sketchy lines are left, and nothing is filled in later.

FOLLOW-UP

I. *Have students write simple sentences using as many of the characters as they can.*
II. *Create a bulletin board display of calligraphy. After you have completed the scroll painting lesson (page 24), students can make a display of both types of artwork.*
III. *Take students to a local museum or use an art book to show them examples of traditional Asian writing tools.*

TOPICS FOR DISCUSSION

How does the beauty and craftsmanship of writing utensils reflect the value placed on writing in China and Japan? ■ Why is the written word and the act of writing itself so important in China and Japan? ■ Discuss the concept of *qi* as expressed in calligraphy. What attitude does it indicate? Does it work for you? How does it work?

NAME CHARACTERS

(Personal Names)   (Family Names)

大 dà (big)	名 míng (reputation, name)	男 nán (male)	德 dé (virtue, power)	昭 zhāo (luminous)	須 Xū	李 Lǐ	敖 Áo
小 xiǎo (small)	明 míng (bright)	女 nǚ (female)	文 wén (lang., lit.)	錦 jǐn (elegant)	余 Yú	毛 Máo	白 Bái
月 yuè (moon)	玉 yù (jade)	兒 ér (son)	平 píng (peace)	敬 jìng (respect)	朱 Zhū	那 Nà	陳 Chén
天 tiān (heaven)	金 jīn (gold)	子 zǐ (child)	愛 ài (love)	琳 lín (gem)	沈 Shěn	區 Oū	杜 Dù
安 ān (peace)	銀 yín (silver)	娘 niáng (girl, woman)	統 tǒng (govern, rule)	麗 lì (beautiful)	林 Lín	潘 Pān	耳 Ěr
好 hǎo (good)	龍 lóng (dragon)	士 shì (scholar)	富 fù (wealth)	祿 lù (prosperity)	候 Hóu	秦 Qín	方 Fāng
美 měi (beautiful)	達 dá (successful)	石 shí (stone)	白 bái (white)	兰 lán (orchid)	范 Fàn	容 Róng	高 Gāo
梅 méi (plum blossom)	清 qīng (clear, pure)	陰 yīn (female, dark)	黑 hēi (black)	凤 fèng (phoenix)	張 Zhāng	宋 Sòng	和 Hé
花 huā (flower)	樂 lè (happiness)	阳 yáng (male, light)	紅 hóng (red, good, luck)	日 rì (sun)	孟 Mèng	唐 Táng	晉 Jìn
宝 bǎo (precious, rare)	力 lì (strength)	英 yīng (brave, bold)	人 rén (person)	荫 yīn (shade)	焦 Jiāo	王 Wang	孔 Kǒng

Scroll Landscape Paintings

CHINA OR JAPAN

CONTEXT

Ink landscape painting is probably the most recognizable art form in Asia. Traditional scroll paintings are popular in both China and Japan. They often feature distant rounded mountains enveloped in mist; rivers and waterfalls; paths and bridges; and boats, houses, and people. The principles behind Asian and Western landscape painting differ greatly. For example, unlike most American painters, a Chinese or Japanese landscape painter:

- paints from memory, not at the site
- paints quickly with no changes
- uses ink on paper or silk
- leaves parts of the painting bare
- includes both nature and some indication of human presence
- mounts the painting on a scroll

This activity acquaints students with the steps involved in Chinese- or Japanese- style landscape painting. Students will come to appreciate the skill of Asian artists when they try painting a landscape on paper without first sketching a rough draft. Begin this activity by studying the principles of Chinese or Japanese landscape painting. Because it uses the same materials and techniques as writing, this project works best if it follows the lesson on calligraphy (page 20).

DIRECTIONS

1. Put a small amount of liquid ink into several small paper cups (one cup for each group of two or three students). Pour a small amount of water into another cup. As in the calligraphy activity, students need to dip their brush pen first in water, wiping it off on the edge of the cup, and then dip it in the ink, wiping it off again to remove any excess liquid.

MATERIALS

- off-white drawing paper (8 1/2 by 18 inches or 12 by 24 inches)
- brush pens, one for each student, and black ink
- contrasting colored construction paper for mounting (12 by 35 inches or 16 by 35 inches)
- small paper cups, 1 for every 2 or 3 students
- glue or paste
- book of Chinese art (from Mustard Seed Garden) or samples of Chinese paintings
- practice paper

2. On practice paper, students can begin experimenting with the brush pen and ink. Encourage them to draw a variety of mountains, bodies of water, buildings, bridges, and boats. Explain that they can use this paper to try any ideas that they might want to include on their final painting.

3. When the class is ready, distribute the drawing paper. Do not allow students to sketch in pencil first, because this undermines the conventions of Chinese painting. Before starting, the children should try their best to get a mental image of what they want to paint. Since no changes are permitted, students will need to begin again if they make a mistake.

4. After the paintings have dried, students need to mount their artwork. Glue should be applied sparingly and evenly to the back of the paper. The painting should be placed on the construction paper so that the space at the top is twice that at the bottom. Explain to the class that this is supposed to represent the ratio of heaven to earth as we view it here on earth.

5. Encourage students to make up poems about their artwork. Because they are considered part of the painting, the poems should be included in one corner of the paper.

6. Have students select a Chinese name and create a name chop or seal (page 26). Traditionally, this seal is stamped on the painting, near the poem.

T E A C H I N G   T I P S

Emphasize the importance of tradition in Chinese landscape painting. Although students should be encouraged to create their own artwork, stress the need to observe the conventions of scroll landscape painting. There is sometimes a fine line between creativity and inaccuracy.

■

Point out that not all areas of the paper should be covered. Use examples of Chinese or Japanese paintings to show the creative use of blank spaces—how the mind fills that space in, assigning it as sky, river, or mist, even though nothing is there.

■

On Chinese paintings, the poems are written vertically. Students can write in English horizontally in a blank space near the top.

■

Cleanup is essentially the same as for calligraphy (see page 20).

■

FOLLOW-UP

I. *To make a real scroll painting, attach a dowel to the bottom of the mounting paper. After securing a flat stick at the top, attach a piece of string to the stick for hanging.*
II. *Hang a scroll painting (with or without the dowels) in a special area of your classroom. Place a flower arrangement underneath (page 38). The Japanese call this kind of area a* tokonoma. *Change the painting regularly so that everyone's artwork can be displayed.*

Name Chops

CHINA

CONTEXT

In China people stamp their name chop in the same way that Americans write their signature. For example, every time someone in China withdraws money from a bank, legalizes a contract, picks up a registered letter, or finalizes a legal document, he or she must stamp a name chop. Similarly, artists and calligraphers use a name chop as proof of authenticity.

A name chop is made up of three parts: the material being carved, such as stone, ivory, or wood; the characters engraved on the chop itself; and the red paste used for stamping. Because they are carved by hand, the density of the material affects the difficulty of engraving. Jade, for example, is extremely hard and time-consuming to inscribe.

By selecting a Chinese name and making their own name chop, students will learn that in China, the family name always comes first and that personal names, which usually consist of one or two characters, are chosen to reflect desirable qualities in a child.

DIRECTIONS

1. Instruct students to select a Chinese name from the chart on page 23. Though not required, it is customary to choose a family name that begins with the same letter as your own last name.

Although there are no fixed personal names in China, some characters are used for boys, while others are traditionally given to girls. In general, names of flowers or gemstones are reserved for girls, while characters for qualities such as boldness and courage tend to be given to boys. The character "yang" is associated with boys, while the character "yin" is associated with girls. It is important for students to feel that the name they select reflects their particular goals, such as *Yingshi,* or Bold Scholar.

MATERIALS

+ chart of common Chinese names (page 23)
+ tracing paper
+ red acrylic paint or a red ink pad
+ flat plastic trays or stiff, non-absorbent boards
+ small brayers (hand rollers)

Method I

+ "safety cut" or art gum erasers ("safety cut" erasers work best but they're fairly expensive)
+ small blade linoleum cutters

Method II

+ Styrofoam rectangles
+ pen points
+ knives

Remind students that the family name always comes first and that it is common to use a single character for them. While most personal names use two characters, one-character names are also fairly common. Today in China, when names are written in the Latin alphabet, the last name is written first, followed by two personal names written together as one word, for example, Deng Xiaoping. Clearly, the seals are easier to make if the characters are not too complicated.

2. Once students have selected their names, they need to trace the characters on paper. Depending on the shape of the seal, they should put the family name on top with the two personal names lined up below, or put the family name on the right side and the two characters for the personal name, one above the other, on the left side. Tell students to *reverse the tracing paper* and put it on top of the eraser or Styrofoam square.

3. To make a rubbing, instruct students to follow one of the two methods described below.

   Method I: Use small linoleum cutters to carve the characters into the eraser. On the back of the seal, mark which side is up with an arrow.

   Method II: Use a pen point to cut dots into the Styrofoam along the lines of the characters. Then use a knife to connect the dots, making a sharp image. Again, indicate which side is up on the back of the seal.

4. Spread red acrylic paint evenly onto plastic trays. Students should press their seals onto the trays or run the inked brayer over the seal. The seal can then be stamped. Encourage students to test their name chop by pressing it down on scrap paper. If it is not clear, they should etch the lines more deeply. Alternatively, suggest using a red ink pad. The latter is easier to handle and tends to make a finer print, although the color is not as bright.

TEACHING TIPS

Although erasers are more expensive than Styrofoam, the quality of the name chop will be significantly better.

■

Spend some time talking to your students about the proper use of linoleum cutters or knives. Given the level of your class, you might consider having students do everything *except* the carving. You would then be the master carver.

■

Sometimes when students stamp their name chop on a painting (or another finished product), the impression is not sharp. Encourage them to stamp another piece of colored paper until the image is just the way they want it. They can then carefully cut out the stamp and paste it neatly on their painting.

■

FOLLOW-UP

I. *Instruct students to cooperate to create a dictionary of their new names. On blank index cards, have them write down their Western name followed by their new Chinese name and its English translation, and stamp their name chop at the bottom. You might want to post the cards around the classroom.*

II. *Allow students to stamp other schoolwork with their name chop. (Keep a red ink pad handy. It's quicker and easier than the paint.)*

III. *Name chops were the forerunners of printing. Initiate a class discussion about the similarities between using a name chop and printing.*

Writing Names in Katakana

JAPAN

CONTEXT

apanese is one of the most complex languages in the world. It consists of two basic types of script: Kanji and Kana.

Kanji are Chinese characters. The term "character" is used for the ideographs that comprise the Chinese written language. Each character has meaning, for characters are symbols used to represent ideas. Originally pictographs or pictures, they have been modified to become the forms used today. Despite the complete dissimilarity between their spoken languages, Japan borrowed this form of writing from China in ancient times, about 1,500 years ago. Although the number of characters used in modern Japanese is limited, characters are still an integral part of the written language.

Most Japanese names are written in *kanji*. The family name, which usually consists of two to three characters, is written first. This is followed by the personal name, which may consist of one to three characters.

Kana, or syllabary, are forms adapted from Chinese characters about a thousand years ago. These forms have no meaning in themselves. They are used purely to represent sounds. *Kana* are symbols that represent a syllable, in most cases a consonant plus a vowel. In contrast, the letters in the alphabet we use represent just a consonant or a vowel. Note that in Japanese, the five vowels sounds—ah, ee, oo, eh, oh—are considered syllables.

Kana, itself, takes two forms. One, *hiragana*, is used for Japanese words. The other, *katakana*, is used for foreign words or to show the pronunciation of proper names.

Because it is used for foreign words and phrases, your students should learn to write their own names in *katakana*. Explain to the class that since Japanese has many fewer sounds than English, the English sounds will sometimes have to be changed or adapted. The sound "tee," for example, is written using the syllabary "te + i."

By translating their own names into *katakana*, students will learn not only how the Japanese language uses syllabary rather than letters to represent consonants and vowels, but the form of *katakana* syllables as well.

TIP

Focus on first names because last names tend to be complicated. However, if ambitious students want to convert their full name, encourage them to try.

■

ア a	イ i	ウ u	エ e	オ o	カ ka	キ ki	ク ku	ケ ke	コ ko
サ sa	シ shi	ス su	セ se	ソ so	タ ta	チ chi	ツ tsu	テ te	ト to
ナ na	ニ ni	ヌ nu	ネ ne	ノ no	ハ ha	ヒ hi	フ fu	ヘ he	ホ ho
マ ma	ミ mi	ム mu	メ me	モ mo	ヤ ya	ユ yu	ヨ yo		
ラ ra	リ ri	ル ru	レ re	ロ ro	ワ wa	ヲ o	ン n		
ガ ga	バ ba	パ pa	キャ kya	キュ kyu	キョ kyo	シャ sha	シュ shu	チャ cha	
ザ za	ジ ji	ズ zu							
ダ da	ヂ ji	ヅ zu	デ de						

DIRECTIONS

1. Discuss the meaning of syllabary.

2. Distribute charts of *katakana* to your students. Go over the pronunciation of each sound. Point out that vowel sounds in Japanese are the same as in Spanish or Italian.

3. Use your own name as an example to show students how to convert an English-language name into Japanese. For example: Diana = da/i/a/na. In Japanese this would be written as four *katakana* symbols.

4. Give students enough time to work out their names in *katakana*. They can check with classmates to see if they have arrived at the correct pronunciation.

5. Have them write their *katakana* name on 3- by 5-inch index cards. *Katakana* is either written from left to right, or from top to bottom.

FOLLOW-UP

I. *Suggest that students use their* katakana *name on all class work.*

II. *Post the names on the bulletin board for everyone to see.*

MATERIALS

+ chart of *katakana* syllabary (above)

+ paper with boxes for practice

+ 3- by 5-inch blank index cards

Crests and Banners

JAPAN

CONTEXT

Historians consider the medieval period in Japanese history, which dates from the twelfth to the seventeenth centuries, to be of great significance. Many characteristics of modern Japan date back to that period. In the years prior to 1600, Japan was governed by a feudal system. Powerful clans vied for power, frequently resorting to armed conflict. As in feudal Europe, lords—known as *daimyo* in Japan—built castles to defend their territory and to serve as a base when attacking others. The lords, who were identified by their family crest, had retainers called *samurai*, who owed them total loyalty. When studying this period of Japanese history, divide the class into several groups, with each one representing a powerful clan. In this activity students will design a crest that symbolizes their particular group.

DIRECTIONS

1. Each group should select or design an appropriate crest. Simplified natural objects or geometric shapes work best.

2. Have students draw a large circle on the 8- by 11-inch paper. To create the border, they should draw a smaller circle inside the first.

3. Individual designs should be sketched within the inner circle. Although they should reach from one end to the other, the designs need not cover the entire area.

4. Using markers, crayons, colored pencils, or paints, students should color in their artwork. A single color is fine and lines may be highlighted or darkened if desired.

5. Instruct students to draw and color their crest again on the 9- by 12-inch construction paper.

6. Have students cut a V-shape in one end of the 9- by 12-inch paper to make a banner.

7. Crests and banners can be hung from wires stretched across the room or displayed prominently on the bulletin board.

MATERIALS

+ sample crests (page 32)
+ compass or large circular objects
+ sheets of 8- by 11-inch and 9- by 12-inch white or Manila construction paper
+ pencils
+ markers, crayons, colored pencils, or paints
+ scissors

FOLLOW-UP

I. *While studying this period of history, students can be identified by the crests and banners they created.*

II. *Ask the class to look through several pictures of Japanese castles and draw one that they find particularly striking. You might want to hang these drawings alongside the clan banners.*

III. *Have each group put their clan crest on a folder to contain any group work done during this unit of study.*

IV. *Extend what students have been studying in class by assigning each group a related task, such as making woodblock prints (page 33), or investigating a particular aspect of Japanese culture during this period. This research, like many of the other projects described here, can be presented as an oral report.*

TEACHING TIPS

Japanese crests did not use either the quartering system or European symbols of heraldry. Remind students to keep their designs simple.

■

Although this period in Japanese history is marked by intense competition between clans, this need not be mirrored in your classroom. Many clans were allies, so you can be historically correct by asking students to work together peacefully and cooperatively. By choosing clans other than the Tokugawa, you can avoid having one group represent the winner.

■

You may wish to be historically accurate by having the class copy actual Japanese crests. Encourage students to research some of the powerful clans that existed during Japan's medieval period.

■

Crest Templates

Woodblock Prints
CHINA OR JAPAN

CONTEXT

Woodblock printing originated in China. Using techniques employed in carving name chops and steles, the Chinese began engraving wooden printing blocks. Eventually, the process spread to Japan. In both countries, woodblock printing was used for words as well as for pictures.

Japanese woodblock prints are famous around the world. They reached their peak during the Tokugawa period (1600–1868). Famous artists, such as Hiroshige and Utamaro, drew detailed pictures that were then executed by skilled artisans. Although multi-colored prints require a series of perfectly aligned blocks, students can make their own single-color "woodblock" prints very easily.

DIRECTIONS

1. Tell students to draw a picture on a "safety cut" eraser. Remind them that, when printed, their sketch will be the reverse of what they drew on the eraser. Students can also draw the picture on a sheet of paper and transfer the reverse image onto the eraser by making a rubbing of it.

2. Using a fine linoleum cutter, students should carve the lines of their picture.

3. Put some paint on the plastic tray and spread evenly with the roller.

4. Instruct students to neatly cover the carved surface of the eraser with paint.

5. After turning the eraser over on paper, students should press down firmly.

6. The paint will begin to dry as soon as the eraser is removed.

MATERIALS

+ "safety cut" erasers, at least 4 by 4 inches
+ linoleum cutters with fine blades
+ one color of acrylic or tempura paint
+ flat plastic tray
+ brayer or small roller for spreading paint
+ construction paper

FOLLOW-UP

I. *Students can learn more about Japan during the Tokugawa period by carefully examining such prints as those of the Tokaido stations or Edo (present-day Tokyo).*
II. *Use this activity to launch a class discussion about the ways in which printing revolutionized how people learned about their world.*
III. *Woodblock printing was used not only for the written word but also for illustrations, advertisements, and posters. Discuss the artistic methods of creating beautiful prints, as well as their uses. Ask students why they think these prints were so important.*

TIPS

You can make several prints from one eraser. Try varying the color of both the paper and the paint.

■

When displaying students' prints, you might also want to show the "block" carvings.

■

Landscape Gardens

CHINA OR JAPAN

CULTURE

CONTEXT

Chinese gardens, especially those dating back to the Ming dynasty, are world famous. The notion of a small garden imitating the larger physical environment is very ancient, much older in fact than the Ming gardens. For the Chinese, hills, ponds, islands, and rocks had symbolic meanings. These ideas were carried to Japan, where Japanese versions of landscape gardens were constructed based on Chinese models. Today Chinese and Japanese landscape gardens are copied around the world. The idea of a world in miniature is just as appealing today as it was thousands of years ago.

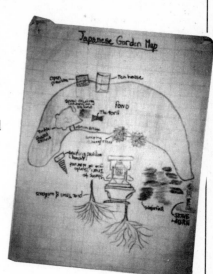

DIRECTIONS

1. Students should locate or construct a wooden or heavy cardboard tray. (Vary the size according to the amount of classroom space.)

2. Distribute as many pictures of landscape gardens as possible, and encourage students to design their garden before beginning. Then have students sketch out their garden either on the tray or on a piece of paper of comparable size. Scale should be part of the planning.

3. Have students use colored plasticine or papier-mâché for the pond, hills, and islands. Other craft materials can be used for the buildings, trees, and bridges.

4. Review the theory behind Japanese landscape gardens.

MATERIALS

+ wood or heavy cardboard tray

+ colored plasticine or papier-mâché

+ other materials for buildings, trees, and bridges (such as cardboard, wood, crepe paper, etc.)

TEACHING TIPS

The ridged side of corrugated cardboard is excellent for replicating tile roofs, most of which are gray. The ridges should always be vertical, never horizontal.

■

Gardens often have buildings with thatched roofs. These can be created by gluing straw or long dried grasses on cardboard. Natural sticks and twigs make great poles for open pavilions.

■

Painting the surface of the water with clear acrylic will make it appear shiny.

■

FOLLOW-UP

Possible research topics:
I. *Compare and contrast Japanese and Chinese landscape gardens.*
II. *Investigate the meaning of several elements in Japanese gardens.*
III. *In addition to the landscape (pond-and-hill garden), find out more about the four other types of Japanese gardens: dry landscape, tea garden, stroll garden, and courtyard garden.*

Zen Dry Landscape Gardens

JAPAN

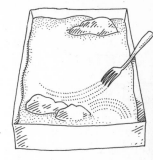

CONTEXT

During the medieval period of Japanese history, a form of Buddhism known as Zen became very influential, especially among the samurai class. Zen emphasized sudden enlightenment, simplicity, and self-discipline. Out of these concepts, an austere aesthetic developed.

Although Zen Buddhism originated in China, it has become closely identified with Japan. The dry landscape garden, which is generally associated with Zen temples, is especially typical of Zen Buddhist aesthetics in Japan. The garden is usually a small area that was originally intended to encourage meditation. Natural objects are simple and suggestive, consisting of gravel or sand raked in special ways as well as some larger rocks and moss. The viewer does not enter the garden; he or she either walks around the outside or admires it from a veranda. Pebbles or sand are used to represent water. Use this activity to reinforce the ideals of the Zen aesthetic or to extend your study of medieval Japan.

DIRECTIONS

1. Obtain or make a tray, approximately 10 by 18 inches (the exact size is not important, but it should be rectangular). The tray must have a rim to keep the gravel from spilling.

2. Completely cover the bottom of the tray with about a 1/2-inch layer of gravel.

3. After studying the picture of a dry landscape, students should discuss these questions: What does the garden represent? Why are the stones located where they are? The purpose of the discussion is to stimulate students to think about the garden that they will create.

4. Students should be able to explain the location of the rocks in their own garden. They should not simply copy the design of the garden they used as a model.

5. Instruct students to use the small rake or fork to arrange the sand in careful geometric patterns. At some gardens, the gravel is raked lengthwise, with a circle around each cluster of stones.

6. Have students write a paragraph explaining the design of their classroom garden.

FOLLOW-UP

I. Possible research topics: *Zen Buddhism* ▮ *Other famous Zen gardens in Japan* ▮ *Origins of Zen Buddhism in China, where it is called Chan Buddhism*

MATERIALS

+ picture of dry landscape garden, such as Ryoan-ji Temple in Kyoto, Japan

+ 10- by 18-inch tray

+ fine white or gray gravel (the kind that goes in fish tanks works well)

+ several rocks of assorted sizes

+ small rake or fork

T I P S

You need clean, unused gravel for the garden, but the stones can be used in a fish tank when the project is dismantled.

▮

Rough-surfaced rocks are better than smooth ones. Make sure students consider scale when adding the rocks.

▮

Noh Mask

JAPAN

CONTEXT

Noh theater is a traditional and highly symbolic form of Japanese drama, dating back about 500 years. Based on Buddhist principles, it features music, dance, elaborate costumes, and masks. The backdrop of the stage is always the same: a pine tree painted on a gold background. No other scenery is used. Even when held in a modern theater, a platform with a cypress bark roof is constructed on the existing stage. There is no curtain. Musicians playing traditional instruments—drum and flute—sit on stage in full view of the audience. A small chorus chants and sings the narration and dialogue. The actors, all of whom are men, wear elaborate and gorgeous robes regardless of the status of the character they represent. In most plays, the main characters all wear masks, which instantly identify each as a demon, an old man, or a woman. Very few props are used; for example, a kimono lying on stage may indicate a sick person. Actions are symbolic: walking in a circle around the stage represents a long journey; the lifting of a hand represents weeping.

When learning about the medieval period in Japanese history, students can study Noh drama as an example of the predominant aesthetic ideal. This form of drama was immensely popular with both the samurai and the aristocracy. Use this activity in conjunction with a study of medieval Japanese culture or as part of a unit on literature.

Real Noh masks are carved from wood and are true works of art. Many museums display old Noh masks as part of their Japanese collections. Have students look at several pictures of Noh masks before they begin.

DIRECTIONS

1. Request a volunteer to be the model for the mask. (You will need a different student for each mask you make.) Cover the student's face completely with a thin layer of petroleum jelly. Make sure that the eyebrows, lashes, and hairline are all covered. Have the student lie down during the initial steps in making the mask. Because the freshly laid plaster gauze will drip, put paper or cloth towels around the student's face and clothes.

2. With *dry* hands, cut the plaster gauze into pieces of different sizes and shapes: some larger, some smaller, and some triangular. Place the cut pieces on a tray near the bowl of water.

MATERIALS

+ plaster gauze (one roll makes 3 or 4 masks)
+ paraffin wax, about two squares for each mask
+ pan or Crock-Pot
+ plasticine or crayons
+ petroleum jelly
+ white glue
+ disposable paint brushes
+ small bowl of water
+ scissors
+ small tray
+ paper or cloth towels
+ newspaper
+ hair dryer (optional)

3. Quickly wet one piece of plaster gauze at a time. Use both hands to tug at the ends in order to release the plaster. Starting with larger pieces, fold lengthwise and place so that the fold serves as an edge. This will keep the ends of the mask from fraying.

4. When applying plaster gauze, work from the outside of the face toward the center. First do the edges around the face. Next do the forehead and cheeks, followed by the chin, nose, and area around the eyes. In general, you will need smaller pieces for the nose and eyes.

5. Lay strips so that they overlap. Use at least two layers for strength and, as you finish, look for places that need extra strips.

6. Be sure the student can breathe easily and is comfortable with the process. *Arrange a signal, such as a raised hand, to indicate you should stop in case the student becomes distressed.*

7. The student must lie still until the plaster has hardened. This usually takes about 15 minutes, but you can speed up the process with a hair dryer. When the plaster feels cold, it is firm and can be removed from the student's face.

8. To facilitate removing the mask, have the student look down at his or her lap and blow out a puff of air. Place your hands on the mask and work it off. If any part breaks, you can patch it.

9. Wait a whole day for the mask to dry completely. Put crumpled newspaper inside to maintain the shape while it is drying.

10. Melt some paraffin wax in a pan or Crock-Pot. With a paint or glue brush, apply it onto the mask. It should dry immediately. Note that these brushes cannot be reused.

11. With melted crayons or plasticine, color the mouth and eyebrows. Paint another layer of melted paraffin wax over the entire mask.

12. Paint the inside of the mask with some diluted white glue.

13. Finally, make string holes on both sides of each mask, about an inch from the edge, so they can be worn.

TEACHING TIPS

You can buy paraffin wax from art supply stores or the supermarket. Look in the section where canning supplies are sold.

■

Plasticine works very well for color and is easy to use.

■

Although the paraffin wax gives the mask an attractive translucent quality, you can dispense with it at the end of step #9 if you carefully smooth the plaster while it is still wet. In this case, simply paint the plaster when it has dried completely.

■

Resources
There are excellent video tapes of Noh drama available from both the Japan Society (333 E. 47th St., New York, NY 10017), and the Asia Society (725 Park Ave., New York, NY 10021). In addition, many books have been written on the subject.

■

FOLLOW-UP

I. *Discuss several different styles of theatrical performances. In what ways is Noh different?*
II. *Students can try wearing masks as they perform. What restrictions result? How would that influence an actual performance? Why would people wear masks as part of the dramatic process?*
III. *Have students read one or more translated Noh plays; they are quite short. Discuss the plots and characters. Have students read a Noh play out loud or act it out.*

Flower Arrangement
JAPAN OR CHINA

CONTEXT

The art of flower arranging, which dates back to the Tang dynasty, spread from China to Japan during the seventh century. However, by the 1800s, this elaborate and unique art form had declined in China, while it was still flourishing in Japan. There, flower arranging is based on the aesthetic principles derived from Zen Buddhism. A primary consideration is simplicity, through which the arranger attempts to capture the beauty of nature in a single vase.

Today most people associate flower arranging with Japan. And for good reason. This small island nation is home to nearly 60 different schools of floral design, although only six of these are considered significant. For American students, the Sogetsu School is a good choice to follow; the structure it provides makes simple flower arranging easy. You may wish to do a class demonstration, and then have a different student do an arrangement for the room every few days. You can also make this an individual or group project in which a small number of students demonstrate to the rest of the class.

Principles of Sogetsu Flower Arrangement

You can see from the diagram on page 39 that the Sogetsu School of flower arrangement is based on angles and proportions. There are three main lines or stems: longest (*shin* in Japanese), medium (*soe*), and shortest (*hikae*). Supplemental stems can be cut for the arrangement, but they should always be shorter than the main line they accompany. The description that follows is the most basic type of flower arrangement.

Proportions: The *longest stem* should be one and a half times the measurement of the vase. The vase is measured by adding the diameter to the height. The *medium stem* should be three-quarters the length of the longest stem. The *shortest stem* should be three-quarters the length of the medium stem.

Angles: The *longest stem* is tilted at a 10–15 degree angle from the perpendicular. Tilt either to the left or the right front. The *medium stem* is tilted at a 40–50 degree angle. Tilt in the same direction as the longest stem. The *shortest stem* is tilted at a 75 degree angle. Tilt this stem in the *opposite* direction from the other two.

After the three main stems are in place, you may add supplemental stems as desired. However, avoid crowding. The simpler the lines, the more

PROPORTIONS

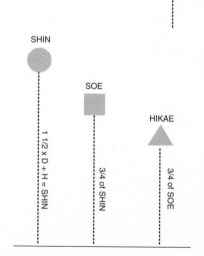

effective the arrangement. In general, Japanese arrangers use far fewer flowers than their Western counterparts.

Try using branches for the longest and medium stems, and flowers for the shortest and its supplemental stems.

TECHNIQUES

Cutting: Cut flower stems horizontally at the end. Cut branches at an angle.

Trimming: All bruised or torn flowers should be trimmed. Also trim any branches that cross each other. Unnecessary branches should be trimmed and leaves thinned out to avoid obscuring the lines of the stem.

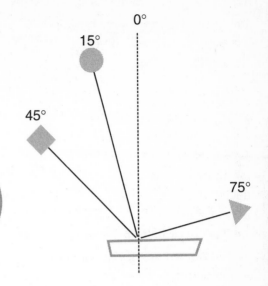

Adding plant material: Position branches into a flower pin *(kenzan)*, tilting them to the desired angle. If a stem is too thin, try cutting a small segment of a larger one from another branch and inserting the smaller stem into it. Then position securely in the flower pin. The flower pin should always be placed to one side of the vase, never directly in the center.

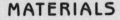

MATERIALS

+ 3–6 flowers, of 1 or 2 varieties
+ 2–4 branches of a bush or tree, comparatively straight and not too brittle
+ flat flower vase or attractive bowl
+ flower pin
+ flower clippers, garden clippers, or strong scissors
+ water

DIRECTIONS

1. Trim all branches and flowers according to the principles of Sogetsu flower arrangement.

2. Take one of the branches and measure it against the dimensions of the vase. Cut to size.

3. Cut the second branch to three-quarters the size of the first.

4. Cut one of the flowers to three-quarters the size of the second.

5. Position the flower pin in the vase.

6. Place each plant in the flower pin according to the directions above.

7. Cut two or three more flowers to supplement the third main stem. You may use a few leaves to conceal the flower pin, but be careful not to crowd or clutter the arrangement.

8. Add any supplemental stems sparingly.

9. Add water until the flower pin is completely covered.

10. Place the vase asymmetrically on an attractive mat or flat piece of wood.

FOLLOW-UP

I. *Create a* tokonoma. *A* tokonoma *is a niche or corner in a traditional Japanese home where objects of beauty are displayed. Most commonly, a scroll painting is hung on the wall and a flower arrangement is placed beneath. Create a* tokonoma *in your classroom by first setting aside a place in the room, such as the top of a bookshelf. Hang a scroll painting (page 24) above a fresh flower arrangement. One or two students can be responsible for changing the* tokonoma *at a set interval.*

II. **Possible research topics:** *Flower arranging in China, Principles of Japanese flower arranging and the development of different schools*

TEACHING TIPS

The wide top of a flat or low vase (as opposed to a bottle or a cylinder-shaped container) makes arranging and balancing easier. If no vase is available, look for an attractive soup bowl or even a cake pan.

■

The flower pin (*kenzan* in Japanese) is essential for securing the flowers and branches. Most florist shops carry them and they are not too expensive. Caution students to use care when handling a flower pin because fingers can get punctured.

■

You will need clippers or strong scissors to cut flowers and branches to the desired height and to trim off excess foliage.

■

Some florists believe that flower stems should always be cut under water. Others disagree. Since it is easier for students to cut the stems dry, that approach is recommended.

■

A variety of items can be placed under the vase. For example, a bamboo or straw place mat, a flat piece of wood attractively finished, or even a flat section of tree trunk or twigs tied together serve the purpose. Whatever the material you choose, it should be natural and flat enough for the vase to rest on without tipping.

■

Resources

Each of the major Japanese schools of flower arrangement has a link listed at the Culture: Hobby: Art of Flower Arrangement Web site. Go to http://www.jinjapan.org/jd/org/006028173.html.

■

New Year's Celebration
CHINA

CONTEXT

Traditionally China has used a lunar calendar in which the months of the year are determined by the cycle of the moon. For example, the first of the month is always a crescent, while the middle of the month is a full moon. Today the Chinese plan their everyday activities according to the solar calendar, just as we do in the United States. However, traditional festivals and holidays are still determined by the lunar calendar. As a result, the day they occur on the solar calendar changes from one year to the next.

The lunar New Year is the most important day of the year in China. Chinese people living in other countries remember the customs of their homeland by celebrating this holiday as well. Before the special day, houses are carefully cleaned and decorated, special foods are prepared, debts are paid, and firecrackers are set off. Most Chinese try to go home to be with their families. Holiday decorations include imitation firecrackers, lucky characters, and cut paper designs. Most businesses are closed for at least a few days. The Lantern Festival, which marks the end of the New Year season, is celebrated on the fifteenth day of the lunar New Year, at the time of the first full moon. Children march in elaborate processions carrying brightly-colored lanterns.

According to the Chinese Zodiac, each year of a 12-year cycle is associated with a particular animal. For example, 1990 was the year of the horse and 1995 was the year of the pig. Some people believe that an individual's personality and fortune are determined by the characteristics of the animal representing their birth year.

Firecrackers

The Chinese invented gunpowder, the ingredient that makes firecrackers explode. Traditionally, it was believed that the noise from bursting firecrackers would frighten off evil spirits. So it was especially important to set them off at the beginning of a new year.

Pretend firecrackers are a common decoration of the New Year season. Use long bunches of them to decorate your classroom. They add a decidedly festive air.

DIRECTIONS

1. Cover toilet tissue spools with red paper. Glue the seam and tuck in the ends.

2. Decorate with gold or silver paint.

3. Glue a loop of red construction paper on one end.

4. Attach each firecracker to one link in a red construction paper chain. Make the chains as long or short as you need.

MATERIALS

+ red tissue paper
+ toilet tissue spools
+ gold and silver paint (half-pint cans are more than enough for the entire class)
+ gold paper
+ cardboard
+ red construction paper
+ glue and scissors

5. At the top of the chain, attach either a cutout of a lucky character or a cardboard circle that is covered in gold paper and decorated.

6. Attach a loop at the top for hanging. Strings of firecrackers can be hung near the door or from the ceiling.

Lucky Characters

Lucky characters are those that are identified with desirable qualities. For example, the characters for wealth, good fortune, a long life, and prosperity are all considered lucky. Spring, the season ushered in by the Chinese New Year, is considered a lucky character because it symbolizes renewal and good times. Many of these characters have homophones. For example, the word for bat is a homophone for wealth and good fortune. The word for deer is a homophone for prosperity. Over the years, pictures of these animals have become symbols of the qualities themselves. Encourage students to find or draw pictures of some of these homophonic animals.

DIRECTIONS

Provide students with the following instructions:

1. In gold ink, write several lucky characters on squares of red paper.

2. Hang some of them upside down. The Chinese word *dao* means both "upside down" and "arrived." When a lucky character is placed upside down, it means that the lucky wish will arrive. Display a note explaining why the character is hanging upside down.

MATERIALS

✦ list of lucky characters (below)

✦ red construction paper

✦ gold ink

lù - prosperity   shòu - long life   fù - wealth   chūn - spring   fú - happiness, good fortune

Lanterns

As you read on page 41, decorative lights are a special part of the Lantern Festival, the celebration that occurs two weeks after the Chinese New Year. Lanterns, representing the first full moon of the lunar calendar, add to the holiday spirit. They are also very easy to make.

DIRECTIONS

Provide students with the following instructions:

1. Fold the construction paper in half horizontally.

MATERIALS

✦ red construction paper

✦ gold and silver paint

✦ glue and scissors

✦ strips of paper shorter than the construction paper

2. Cut parallel slits from the fold, upward and downward, to about two inches from the edge. (See diagram at right.) Open the paper so the fold bulges toward you.

3. After decorating with gold and silver paint, cut fancy designs into the slats.

4. Connect the right and left sides of the paper to make a cylinder, with the decorated side facing out.

5. Glue two paper strips inside as braces so the lantern will bulge out. Cement the seam.

6. Put a construction paper loop at the top.

7. Display the lanterns around the room or carry in a Chinese New Year's parade.

HOW TO MAKE A LANTERN

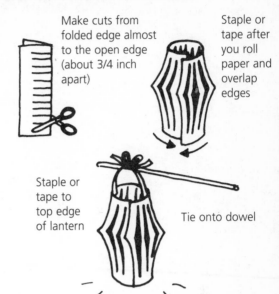

Fold this long side over to the other side.

Make cuts from folded edge almost to the open edge (about 3/4 inch apart)

Staple or tape after you roll paper and overlap edges

Cut a strip of paper from another piece of construction paper about 3/4" x 11"

Staple or tape to top edge of lantern

Tie onto dowel

The Chinese Zodiac

DIRECTIONS

1. Divide the circle of cardboard into 12 equal segments. Outline each pie-shaped wedge in black.

2. On each wedge, write in order the names of the animals listed below and the corresponding years. Then have students draw or paste a picture of that animal if there is room.

3. Place the circle on top of the oak tag. Make a small hole in the center of the cardboard circle and attach the brass fastener by pushing it through the hole and fastening it to the bottom of the oak tag.

4. On the top of the oak tag, write

   **THE CHINESE ZODIAC
   IN WHAT YEAR WERE YOU BORN?**

   Also, draw a large arrow pointing back at the circle. Students can turn the top circle until the arrow points to their correct birth year. Then they can read the information without turning their head sideways.

5. Finally have students draw or cut out a picture of the animal representing their birth year.

MATERIALS

+ large circle of cardboard covered with white paper or painted white
+ large oak tag, preferably red
+ brass fastener
+ thin black marker, colored markers, or paint
+ ruler and protractor

Zodiac Animal	Year of Birth				
Rat	1948	1960	1972	1984	1996
Ox	1949	1961	1973	1985	1997
Tiger	1950	1962	1974	1986	1998
Rabbit	1951	1963	1975	1987	1999
Dragon	1952	1964	1976	1988	2000
Snake	1953	1965	1977	1989	2001
Horse	1954	1966	1978	1990	2002
Sheep	1955	1967	1979	1991	2003
Monkey	1956	1968	1980	1992	2004
Rooster	1957	1969	1981	1993	2005
Dog	1958	1970	1982	1994	2006
Pig	1959	1971	1983	1995	2007

Paper Cutting
CHINA

CONTEXT

The art of paper cutting dates back to the invention of paper in the Han dynasty (206 B.C.–220 A.D.). At first, paper was expensive and cutting was a pastime of noble ladies. However, as it came to be used more widely, the art of paper cutting spread. The finest examples are exquisitely detailed and even multi-colored. For these designs, both scissors and knives are used. However, even simple paper cuts are attractive and enjoyable. They make good decorations for walls or windows, and can be even made into bookmarks. Paper cuts are often created for the Chinese New Year.

DIRECTIONS

Provide students with the following instructions:

1. Fold the paper squares diagonally to make a triangle.

2. Fold again at right angles to make a small triangle that is four layers thick.

3. Sketch a design first or cut freehand. Be sure to cut through all four layers at once. The more intricate the design, the more interesting the paper cut. You may cut along folds or along the outside of the design. If you cut along the folds, be careful to keep them connected.

4. Unfold carefully, one fold at a time. If the design doesn't please you, refold and continue cutting.

5. Press the completed design flat.

6. Mount on contrasting colored paper or attach to a window without mounting.

MATERIALS

+ colored paper squares, not construction paper (origami paper is best)
+ contrasting squares of paper or construction paper
+ scissors
+ glue

TIP

If you are using this activity for the Chinese New Year, use red or gold.

■

FOLLOW-UP

I. Have students create their own bookmarks. They will need to make paper cuts that are much longer than they are wide.
Instruct students to mount on long, narrow strips of paper. Laminate the strips. If desired, students can punch a hole in the top and attach a small ribbon.
II. Use paper cuts to show the plot of a story the class has read. Decide how many incidents in the plot you want to depict (six is usually a good number). Then divide the class into groups to create paper cuts for each incident. You can display the story cuts as a story line with individual captions.

Jade Carving
CHINA

CONTEXT

In China, jade is the most desirable of all gemstones. There are actually two kinds of jade—nephrite and jadeite. Both are poor conductors of heat, feel slightly oily to the touch, produce a bell-like sound when tapped, and are extremely difficult to carve. Over the years, this stone has been used for ritual articles, weapons, tools, jewelry, musical instruments, and bells. Second only to diamonds in hardness, jade has been carved by Chinese artisans since before written history.

Although most people think of jade as being green, the stone is available in a wide range of colors. In addition to several shades of green, it comes in white (like camphor, old snow, and mutton fat) as well as gray, red, pink, yellow, blue, purple, black, or brown.

DIRECTIONS

1. Demonstrate the proper use of plastic knives.

2. Provide each student with a piece of soap. To duplicate the jade carver's art, students should first design their carving on paper, with the "raw material" placed in front of them. Animals in a prone position work well, as do shallow bowls.

3. Have students use a plastic knife to create the basic shape. Have them work on paper towels to catch the soap pieces and shavings.

4. An assortment of other utensils can be used to create fine details. Linoleum cutters, retracted pen points, and pencils all serve as good tools. If linoleum cutters are used, be sure that students know how to operate them safely.

5. Tell students to run their sculptures under water just long enough to smooth the edges. Completed carvings should be put on a paper towel to dry.

MATERIALS

✢ green soap (other colors can also be used)

✢ plastic knives and assorted other utensils

✢ paper towels

✢ paper and pencils

FOLLOW-UP

I. *Create an imaginary museum of jade sculptures and other art projects connected with your study of Chinese culture. Have students write explanatory cards for each artifact.*

II. *Provide students with the opportunity to examine some Chinese jade objects, either in real life or in books. Combine this project with a field trip to a local museum that features Asian art.*

III. *Many other cultures have carved jade. Compare jade carvings in China with those found in Mesoamerica. What are the differences and similarities? How did each society view jade?*

T I P S

Try cutting bars into different sizes. Ask students to choose the piece they prefer.

■

Have the children put their initials on the bottom of the sculpture after they have washed it so their name won't get washed away.

■

Newspapers

JAPAN OR CHINA

CONTEXT

In this activity, students create their own newspaper based on either a work of literature or a period of history that they have recently studied. The project not only helps students learn more about newspapers and journalism, but also tests their understanding of the material that has been covered. Most students enjoy demonstrating what they have learned in such a creative way.

Preparation for this activity provides an excellent opportunity to study newspapers. If your students are already familiar with this topic, you might want to skip the preparation section below.

The Osaka Beat

1795 · "Woodblock printing at its Best" · 2 sen

Saburo Strikes Once Again
by Ben Ji

Saburo and a gang of night rovers stole from the wealthiest man in Osaka, yesterday, at about 4:38 in the morning.

The man robbed, Haru Shutaro, 65, contacted local police. "They ran into my house, threatening to kill me unless I gave them my food," he said. "What could I do?"

The night rovers and Saburo, a man who is well known for stealing food from the rich, ran away too quickly for the police to catch up to them. It was recorded that they went in the house at 4:38, and left at 4:39.

Yoshida*, a master puppeteer at the Hanaza Bunraku Theater, was asked what he knew of this man, since he had visited the theater before.

"Saburo has done this again?" he asked angrily. "When will he ever learn? Stealing is not good, not for the rich or the poor! He is a disgrace to Japan and I wish

he would leave these people alone and let them live in peace!"

Haru later stated: "I wish Saburo were dead! Now I have to find more food to feed my children's mouths. Saburo has lost all face and does not deserve to live here!"

The police seem to agree with him. "I hate that man! He stole all of our clothes just to use it against us!" The Chief of Police angrily yelled. "I hate that man."

What Saburo actually did was steal the police officers' uniforms in order to break into a house and steal food. He and the night rovers did this long before this time, so Saburo has been doing this for a long time.

As you can tell, there is much hatred towards Saburo. But what is wrong with stealing from the rich to feed the poor?

"I do not think that there is anything wrong with it," Yoshida Kinshi, Yoshida's son, said. "He's doing this to help other people survive. If they need food, they

————————————————

Editorial Staff:
Editor-in-chief: Daiana
Assistant editor: Sanji

PREPARATION

I. *List the parts of a newspaper on the chalkboard (news stories, editorials, letters to the editor, feature stories, and classified ads are some). Elicit this information from students as much as possible.*

II. *Discuss the specific characteristics of each type of newspaper article that you listed.*

III. *In order to help students get a better understanding of a news article, have them clip out the headline and first paragraph of a recent story and paste it on a sheet of paper. Then ask the class a series of questions based on the information contained in the article. Usually the first paragraph of a news article answers the questions* Who? What? Where? *and* When?

IV. *As a writing assignment, give students a made-up headline. Ask them to write the first paragraph. Remind the class that in the first paragraph of a news article, the reporter provides the information on who, what, where, and when.*

V. *Ask each student to select a partner. Make sure that after reading each other's first paragraph, they can answer the questions* Who? What? Where? *and* When?

DIRECTIONS

1. Explain to students that they will be writing a newspaper based on various people, places, and events that they have studied.

2. Provide a list of suggestions for different kinds of articles. For example, suggestions based on *The Master Puppeteer* might be

- news articles on the latest adventures of Saburo
- letters to the editor or editorials about conditions at the time (hunger, homelessness, night rovers)

MATERIALS

+ Using a computer program that produces a newspaper format will make this activity more realistic for students. Otherwise you can design your own newspaper.

- theater review of the latest performance of *bunraku* at Hanaza (particularly the new play by Okada)
- other news articles concerning historic events
- appropriate classified ads
- food or restaurant reviews

3. Encourage students to use their imagination to come up with additional articles. Have them check their local newspaper for ideas.

4. Allow students to work in pairs, although each child must write his or her own article.

5. Tell students to submit a brief description of the content and type of article they will be writing. This will ensure a well-balanced newspaper. Remind students to proofread what they have written.

6. Finally, explain to the class that individual articles will be assembled to create a realistic newspaper.

FOLLOW-UP

I. *Hold a class contest for the name of the newspaper and the design of its masthead. Post entries and have students vote by secret ballot.*

II. *Make plenty of copies of the finished newspaper so all students and interested adults can have their own copy.*

III. *Encourage students to design a bulletin board display, preferably in a public place, where their newspaper can be shared with the community. Have them fill up any remaining space with other class work that relates to the novel or historical period being studied.*

TEACHING TIPS

Have a list of suggestions handy for the students who need help.

■

You might want to guide students to the type of article that you think will be most suitable. If you have doubts about what a particular child intends to do, have him or her submit a first draft.

■

Before students begin writing, it is often helpful to review guidelines for appropriate content and language. You might want to compare articles in a reputable newspaper with those found in a supermarket tabloid.

■

Anachronisms are often great sources of fun in a newspaper such as this. Encourage students to think about the level of technology during the period in question. In fact, the very idea of this type of newspaper is anachronistic. Use your judgment about what to allow. In general, look for anything that shows an understanding of the particular time period involved.

■

Encourage students to draw cartoons, especially political ones, for the class newspaper. In some cases, that might be the most appropriate form of expression. In others, suggest that students write a caption to accompany their cartoon.

■

This type of writing, while less structured than an essay, can be equally revealing about a student's comprehension, organization, and writing ability. You might want to use this activity as a substitute writing assignment.

■

Face Painting and Chinese Opera

CHINA

CONTEXT

Although this activity is exciting and enjoyable for most students, it is intended not as an end in itself, but as an integral part of your study of Chinese opera. Before beginning this activity, it is helpful to spend some time reviewing the principles of Chinese theater with the class. Students should get the opportunity to read an actual libretto or play and see either a video or live performance.

In typical American theatrical productions, the stage is an area of illusion or make-believe. The drama being performed tries to represent a time and place different from that of the audience. Viewers are usually cut off from the stage by a curtain. In addition, certain techniques (makeup, costumes, setting, and lighting) perpetuate that illusion, while the actors behave as if the audience did not exist. This kind of production is sometimes referred to as "representational theater."

In Asia, on the other hand, popular productions are viewed as "presentational theater."* Here, the actors remain performers. Makeup, costumes, and backdrops are not realistic. The stage is not disguised for acting, nor is it cut off from theatergoers. Time and place are the same for both actors and audience. Gestures and movements are intended to appeal to viewers and not necessarily to fellow performers.

CHARACTERISTICS OF CHINESE THEATER

In China, a form of theater known as Chinese or Beijing opera developed over the years. The word "opera" indicates that songs are interspersed with dialogue in the play. Beijing opera uses the dialect of Chinese spoken in Beijing, or what is now known as standard Chinese.

The following is a brief outline of several aspects of Chinese opera and what they mean.

Song and Speech Only the clown or fool speaks in a natural voice. Other actors speak in a somewhat distorted or stylized way. It is actually rhythmic, rhymed, and metered speech, the pitch and tempo of which depend on the situation. Singing is interspersed throughout the performance.

Orchestra Clearly visible to the audience is a musical ensemble that includes percussion instruments such as drums, wooden clappers, and cymbals, as well as wind and string instruments. The orchestra, which accompanies all the songs, highlights the action, delineates acts and scenes, emphasizes fighting, and announces the entrance of an important character.

Action Actors use symbolic actions and mime when they walk or move their hands. For example, an actor never "sleeps," but rather puts his

*Presentational theater also exists in the West.

head on his arm. Perfectly timed rhythmic swaying conveys the feeling of being on a boat. Some of the most exciting scenes are those with fighting where battles are accomplished by acrobatic feats and mock swordplay between individuals on stage.

Scenery and Props Most props consist of a table and chairs. These are used to represent a multitude of objects. In addition, there are many conventions that are familiar to Chinese audiences. For example, a piece of black cloth painted with white lines and attached to two bamboo poles is the city wall. Carrying a stick adorned with tassels means an actor is riding a horse. If he throws down the stick, he is dismounting. An oar represents a boat. Two flags with wheels painted on them stand for a chariot. White paper tied to a stick is snow.

Costumes Although costumes are gorgeous and elaborate, they do not vary greatly from one opera to the next. Costumes are intended to indicate the rank of the character that an actor is portraying. For example, high-heeled shoes represent high rank. Colors are also symbolic. Yellow stands for the imperial family, brown or gray for the aged, red or blue for an honest man, and black for one with an unpredictable temper.

Face Painting Of all the unique characteristics of Chinese opera, the most spectacular are the painted faces of the actors. Although the hero and heroine wear a special pink and white makeup and the fool or clown is instantly identifiable by an inverted white triangle covering his eyes and nose, it is the actors with elaborately painted faces that are most unique.

In Chinese theater, the face immediately provides a clue to the character being portrayed. For example, black represents an honest, tough warrior, while white is reserved for someone treacherous and power hungry. Red indicates bravery and loyalty, while blue tells of cruelty. Mixed colors suggest a despicable rogue or a very complex character. And gold or silver denotes the supernatural.

Clearly, Chinese theater appeals with both sight and sound. It is intended as a spectacle, rather than as a realistic representation of some aspect of life. The Chinese audience goes to be entertained, not to ponder the deep underlying message of the playwright.

BEFORE YOU BEGIN

Students should read an example of Chinese opera as literature. After reading the play, try to obtain a video of the performances for students to watch. (See resources, page 51)

Discuss the idea of colors representing certain human qualities. Encourage students to think of examples they might be familiar with: white = fear, red = anger, and yellow = cowardice. Discuss why particular colors might represent certain qualities. Be particularly sensitive to the color-quality equation of black as something bad. Discuss whether there is any logical basis for color-quality equations, or whether the equations are arbitrary. From their study of Chinese opera, students should realize that these equations are completely culture-based. In other cultures, the equations are different.

MATERIALS

+ paper
+ markers, colored pencils, or paints to design faces
+ Caran d'Ache colors (or other brands that are easily removed), especially red, blue, black, gold, and white
+ small paper cups
+ water

DIRECTIONS

Preparation

1. Provide students with a sheet of white paper divided in half and turned so the rectangle is wider than it is long. Instruct them to draw, on each half, an outline of an oval face with only the eyes sketched in. (See diagram, right) Tell students to put their name on both parts of the paper.

2. Instruct the children to write the name of a character from the Chinese opera you have been reading beneath one of the ovals. With the principles of color-coding in mind, they should design and color the face of the featured character. Remind them that their design should reflect the person being portrayed in the play.

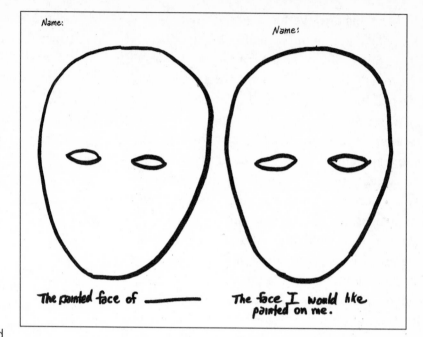

3. Beneath the second oval, have students write the words "The face I would like to have painted on me." They should then design and color a painted face that depicts their own character, also according to the conventions of Chinese opera.

4. Tell students to cut the papers in half, separating their own faces from those representing characters in the play. See Follow-up.

Note: Purists may object to the fact that students are asked to design painted faces for any character of either gender. The goal here is not to re-create Beijing opera, but to help students understand the principles that underlie a different artistic tradition.

Face Painting

1. Students should work in pairs to color each other's face.

2. The painter should keep the picture of the face that he or she is copying near by. If there are any questions, they should be addressed before painting begins.

3. Give each pair of students a small paper cup about half full of water. Distribute Caran d'Ache colors so that each group has a few different shades.

4. Have students dip the stick into the water, applying the wet end to the face.

5. They should apply colors with gentle, even strokes, one color at a time. In most cases, it is not necessary to wait for one color to dry before applying another next to it.

6. When the painters have finished, they should have their faces made up.

FOLLOW-UP

I. *Make a bulletin board display of all the characters from the play you have read. Group all the variations of one character together. When they are assembled, allow students time to examine the differences and similarities. Then lead a discussion about the character and how the class has depicted him or her. Students should rationalize both the similarities and differences that they observe. If certain characters are chosen over others, discuss the reasons for this as well.*

II. *Design another bulletin board display of the faces that students created for themselves. Allow the children to explain why they designed their own faces as they did. (You might want to take notes! This explanation is often very revealing of self-images and ambitions.)*

III. *If possible, have students perform the play they have read, complete with painted faces and costumes. Have different students play the same role in different acts or even scenes. This provides more parts so all students can participate. It also enables the class to be a rotating audience for its own play.*

Some colors are much more popular than others. Red, black, blue, white, and gold are among the most desirable. If you can afford to, buy one of these colors for each pair of students. This will ease the tension of waiting for a particular color that is being used. Other colors are not nearly as popular; you need buy only one or two of these for the whole class. The color sticks should last several years.

■

Prepare one page of face ovals and photocopy the others. Make extras for students who change their minds.

■

If you have an odd number of students, make one group a threesome.

■

Caution students not to leave the Caran d'Ache colors in the cups of water. They will dissolve. Just dip and use.

■

Some children who have sensitive skin may want to wash off their faces very quickly. Keep a mirror in the room so they can look at themselves when they are done. You should try to have a camera handy to snap a photo before the children clean up.

■

Some students might want to keep their face painted for the entire school day. If they will be going to other classes, you should discuss this with your colleagues to make sure that will be all right.

■

Resources

For videos of Chinese operas, contact the Chinese Information and Culture Center, 1230 Avenue of the Americas, New York, NY 10020, or see their Web site http://www.taipei.org/teco/cicc/default.htm. Some libraries also have copies of Chinese opera. If there is a Chinese community in your area, there may be amateur or even professional performances that your students can see.

■

Stick Puppets

CHINA OR JAPAN

CONTEXT

Puppets are an ancient part of drama and make-believe, and they are as varied as the characters they represent. In China and Japan, puppets range from two-dimensional shadow puppets to *bunraku* puppets which are nearly life-size and require three people to manipulate (see page 54).

As people all over the world do, you can use puppets in your classroom to tell stories. Or, if you prefer, you can use them to illustrate only part of a story, such as the characters. A simple stick figure, which can be made in a relatively short amount of time, is well suited for this type of activity.

By manipulating puppets, students can effectively express their opinions on a particular work of literature. Try using them after the class has read several modern Chinese short stories; it's a good way for students to envision a character's appearance and describe their subject either visually or in writing. You will probably want to engage students in a thorough discussion of the literature before beginning this activity.

DIRECTIONS

1. Give students enough time to think about the different characters they have been reading about. Which character do they like best or find most interesting? Have students write a paragraph describing who the character is and explaining why they selected that person. This can be done on a 4- by 6-inch lined index card.

2. After students have finished writing, ask them to reread the sections of the story that deal with their character. When they are finished, they are ready to begin designing their stick puppet.

3. Instruct students to take a large white index card and cut out the shape or outline of the character.

MATERIALS

+ craft sticks, one for each student
+ index cards for each student
+ glue
+ scissors

List A

+ colored pencils
+ crayons
+ markers
+ paints
+ plain pens/pencils
+ chalk, craypas, etc.

List B

+ colored construction paper
+ yarn
+ cloth/felt
+ any other 3-dimensional art materials

4. They need to decorate the cutout, making sure to pay special attention to any important details such as hairstyle and clothing. They should be able to explain their choices using either historical information or examples from the story.

5. Have students use at least two different media in step 4. They may choose one or more items from both List A and List B.

6. Tell students to glue their creation along with the descriptive paragraph onto a craft stick.

FOLLOW-UP

I. Have students share their puppets, explaining why they selected that character and the reasons for its appearance. If several students have created the same character, they can present this information together. They should be able to account for differences in their puppets' appearance.

II. Create a display of the various characters and descriptive cards. Group together all the puppets of a particular story, and, if necessary, all the puppets of the same character. Then have students write a brief summary of the story in which their character appears. It is helpful to post each summary with the corresponding character.

III. Discuss with students why particular characters were more popular with the class than others. Were there any stories from which no characters were chosen? Why was that? Were there some stories that had a number of characters selected? This discussion should help students evaluate an author's skill at characterization.

TEACHING TIPS

Students always like some characters more than others. Usually, this preference varies from one student to the next. Sometimes children find a character fascinating even though they don't approve of his or her actions. Encourage a class discussion about the various characters. It's a good idea not to put restrictions on how many students can select a particular character, but discourage students from copying their friends.

■

Some students like to make a rough outline of their puppet, while others want every curve and detail. Either approach is fine.

■

Reference to the textual material is a crucial part of this activity. Students need to be able to support their conceptualization of what the character looks like. If little or no physical description is provided, the children should use the information they have about people living in China (or Japan) at that time. What kinds of clothes did a person of that status wear? What would their hair look like?

■

Lined 4- by 6-inch and blank 5- by 8-inch index cards are good sizes to use. If you don't have blank cards, turn over the lined ones and use the blank backs.

■

Black yarn is particularly effective for hair. Many students really enjoy cutting cloth to make clothing. Be sure the scissors are sharp enough to cut fabric.

■

Bunraku Puppets

JAPAN

CONTEXT

Bunraku is a type of puppet theater in Japan that dates primarily from the 1700s. The name actually means "literature and music."

There are three components to bunraku: the puppets, a narrator, and a musician. The puppets, which are one half to two-thirds life size, are manipulated by three operators who appear in full view on stage. They consist of the master puppeteer who controls the head and right arm of the figure, the second puppeteer who works the left arm and supplies the props, and the foot manipulator who operates the feet. Although the puppets have moving heads, eyes, eyebrows, mouths, and fingers, there is no body, just traditional clothing over a frame. Female puppets do not have feet due to the length of their kimono; it is the job of the foot manipulator to make it appear as if a woman has legs and feet by moving her clothing in the right way. Numerous props and special effects are also used.

The narrator tells the entire story. He not only takes on the role of each puppet character, but also comments on the events taking place and sings all the poetic parts. The centuries-old language of bunraku plays is not understandable to modern Japanese people; they know the story or use a libretto as in opera. The narrator sits to one side, in full view of the audience. Although he appears to read from a script, he has actually memorized all the lines.

The musician plays a three-stringed instrument called a *shamisen*. Sometimes there are several musicians who accompany the entire performance. The music reflects events in the story and punctuates the action.

For each performance, a stagehand covered in black announces the show. Then the shamisen is played and the narration begins. Only then do the puppets and puppeteers appear. For the first ten minutes, viewers are usually aware of the puppeteers, who appear in full view of the audience. However, within a short time, they become so absorbed in the puppets and their actions that the puppeteers are quickly forgotten. The puppets truly seem to come alive.

Because there is a low wall in front, puppets are held higher than the floor of the stage. This is the "floor level" for the puppets. The master puppeteer wears raised straw clogs while the foot manipulator crouches lower to the ground. They may all appear with black hoods, though famous puppeteers often leave their faces exposed. Although they are not supposed to show expression, their faces somehow seem to reflect the emotions of the puppets.

This project is an adaptation of the elaborate bunraku puppets. You can use it to accompany either a study of Japanese theater, particularly bunraku, or any work of Asian literature.

In order to involve more students, change the puppeteers at each act or scene.

■

Instead of using one narrator, have different students read the voice parts of each character. They can also change at each act or scene.

■

Make several hoods out of black see-through material. Puppeteers should wear their hoods throughout the entire performance.

■

For the stage, use a long table covered with cloth. Remember that the audience shouldn't be able to see behind the stage.

■

Attach a backdrop to the wall behind the stage. In bunraku (unlike noh), the painted curtain is action-specific. However, you can make do with only one by having students paint a natural scene—perhaps cherry blossoms—if that seems appropriate to the play they are performing.

■

DIRECTIONS

Prepare Ahead of Time

1. Make paper templates for the head, neck, torso, arms, and legs. Although real bunraku puppets do not have bodies, they are necessary for this adaptation. Students can cut pieces of cardboard into the desired shapes, especially the oval for the head. Note that all parts are rectangles of different widths and lengths. The arms and legs should be two pieces each, jointed at the elbow and knee with fasteners.

2. Cut out parts for as many puppets as your students will make.

3. Prepare a selection of different kinds of fabric scraps. Make sure that some are large enough to cover the entire body of the puppets, including legs and arms. Colored construction paper or even wallpaper samples will also work.

MATERIALS

+ news board or heavy cardboard
+ paper templates
+ box cutter or "Exacto" knife (for preparation only)
+ scissors
+ glue
+ hole punch
+ round-headed brass fasteners
+ masking tape
+ paint (white, red, black)
+ markers
+ black yarn, medium thickness
+ fabric
+ colored construction paper
+ 2 wooden sticks (or *very* stiff cardboard) for each puppet

INSTRUCTIONS FOR STUDENTS

PART I: Making the Puppet

1. Select rectangles that are the right size for the head, neck, torso, arms, and legs.

2. Cut the corners of the rectangle for the head so it makes an oval shape.

3. Glue the head to the neck and the neck to the torso.

4. Punch holes at the top of each arm rectangle and on each shoulder. Punch two holes at the bottom of the torso and one at the top of each leg rectangle.

5. Attach the arms to the shoulders and the legs to the bottom of the torso, using round-headed brass fasteners.

6. Cut the right arm rectangle in half at the elbow. Punch a hole at the bottom of the upper arm and a corresponding hole at the top of the lower arm. Attach the upper and lower arm together with a brass fastener to make a movable elbow.

7. Tape the fasteners to the back of the puppet.

PART II: Dressing the Puppet

8. Decide what the puppet should be wearing. Select colored paper or fabric and design the costume. Try blending some colors together. If you have to cut fabric, take what you need from the edge, so the rest of the cloth can be used again.

9. Use glue to fasten the costume to the puppet. Be sure that the right arm is able to move.

10. Paint the face and the hands, if visible. Try looking at some pictures of bunraku puppets if you need help.

11. Use black yarn for women's hair. Part it in the middle and make it long. Glue it to the head. Men puppets wear hats.

PART III: Completing the Puppet

12. Attach one stick to the torso of the puppet so it can be held and another stick to the right hand of the puppet so it can be moved.

TEACHING TIPS

Decide ahead of time whether you are going to use this activity for a performance. This will determine which characters your class will need to make.
■

Traditionally, Japanese women wore white face make-up. Even for men, white faces were considered elegant. The type of literature you have chosen will determine whether or not white face paint is appropriate. Be sure to obtain pictures of the kinds of characters that are being portrayed.
■

Making puppets should be a cooperative effort. Groups of two or three students get the most work done in the shortest amount of time.
■

FOLLOW-UP

I. *Use the puppets to perform a play based on a work of literature that the class has read. If you do this, you will also need groups of students to prepare a backdrop and write the script.*

II. *Read* The Master Puppeteer *by Katherine Paterson. This is a good book for the class to read prior to making their puppets.*

Playbills

JAPAN OR CHINA

CONTEXT

Every time you go to the theater, an usher hands you a complimentary Playbill, or the program of the performance. Playbills typically have the logo of the play on the cover. The logo may contain a picture representing an aspect of the play, or it may simply be an attractive way of displaying the title and author. In addition, it lists the cast in the performance, a synopsis of the plot, and information about each of the major performers including the playwright, the director, and the producer.

A Playbill serves as an ideal vehicle for students to display their understanding of a given work of literature. Its format will stimulate class discussion of the structure and performance of a dramatic production. Although Playbills do not necessarily feature comments by theater reviewers, try having students include reviews on the back of their Playbill. This may require students to check newspapers and magazines for the format and content of typical reviews. These activities should take place before students begin work on their own version.

Although this activity can be done with any literature curriculum, it works particularly well with a dramatic presentation. Try incorporating it into your lesson plan if the class is going to read *The Master Puppeteer* by Katherine Paterson. Students can also create their own Playbill for a novel if you translate the plot into the format of a play. Try assigning imaginary or real actors to play the roles of the major characters in the novel. And, instead of having students write descriptive paragraphs about the performers, have them write about the major characters in the book.

DIRECTIONS

1. First students should list the major actors and the roles they play. They will also need to write brief biographies of each character, just as a Playbill includes biographies of the major performers. Have students work out the synopsis, or the summary of the play, in three acts. There can also be a prologue.

2. Students need to fold the 8- by 11-inch or 9- by 12-inch paper in half to form a four-page book.

MATERIALS

✤ scrap paper

✤ 8- by 11-inch or 9- by 12-inch paper

✤ markers, colored pencils, paint, pencils, and pens

✤ an actual Playbill, if possible

3. The front cover should include the Playbill logo as well as the title and author of the play. It should also feature a scene from the play or something suggestive of the content. This is best done in color.

4. The inside of the cover should list the cast and contain the biographies. You can add internal pages as necessary.

5. The synopsis of the play should fill up the remaining three pages. Have students use terms such as Prologue, Act I, and Scene I to make the Playbill realistic.

6. The back cover should contain excerpts of "theater reviews."

FOLLOW-UP

Create a bulletin board display of the playbills so students can share their work with others. If the class actually performs the play, they can use their own Playbills to accompany it.

TEACHING TIPS

If possible, use an actual Playbill as a sample. If you don't have one, ask students if their parents have access to one. Or try your local library or the Internet.

■

Strike a balance between fact (the plot and biographies) and creativity. Try having students who use not only the names of famous theater critics, but also their own names, those of their classmates, and imaginary names appropriate to the story. For the character biographies, encourage students to makeup some colorful, albeit plausible, details.

■

If students want to use a computer, have them print out what they have written and paste it into the Playbill. Or allow them to do the entire Playbill on the computer, with appropriate graphics for the cover.
Just make sure they have a minimum of four pages, including the information specified above.

■

Tea Eggs

CHINA

CONTEXT

Tea eggs are easy to make, good to eat, and beautiful to see. They are also an authentic Chinese snack and breakfast food. They are sold by street vendors as snacks all over China, and often accompany a wholesome breakfast of noodles or grain gruel.

DIRECTIONS

1. Boil all the eggs until they are hard (about 5 minutes).

2. Remove the eggs from the water and allow them to cool.

3. After giving each student a boiled egg, provide the class with the following instructions:

Tap the egg against a tabletop until the shell cracks. Then roll it firmly on a hard surface so all areas of the shell crack but do not come off. Put tea, salt, and anise in the large pot that was used to hard boil the eggs. Using a potholder, carefully pour boiling water over the ingredients. (You might want to assist students with this step.) Place the cracked egg back in the pot. Be sure the eggs are completely covered by the liquid. Simmer the mixture for a full 90 minutes. Allow the eggs to cool. Remove from the liquid and rinse off the tea. Peel the egg and admire its marbled appearance. Then eat and enjoy!

FOLLOW-UP

Discuss why tea eggs are so popular in China. (Point out that tea is the most common beverage in China, and that eggs are inexpensive and nutritious, last longer when boiled, and taste delicious.)

MATERIALS

✤ eggs (one for each child in the class) (This recipe is for a dozen eggs. See Tips for increasing or decreasing the size of the recipe.)

✤ pot large enough to hold all the eggs

✤ 5 tablespoons of loose black tea (orange pekoe)*

✤ 1–2 tablespoons salt

✤ 4 star anise (or 1 teaspoon aniseed)

✤ 3 cups of boiling water

If you can't find loose tea or it's too expensive, open all the tea bags and use the contents.

TIPS

As a math exercise, ask students to calculate the recipe ingredients for more (or fewer) than a dozen eggs.

■

After the eggs are boiled, but before their shells have been cracked, have students write their name or initials on the shell. That way each child can eat the egg that he or she prepared.

■

When students crack the surface of an egg, don't worry if some pieces fall off. It will only result in an egg that is less marbled and more solid brown.

■

Sushi

JAPAN

CONTEXT

Sushi is a delicacy has been eaten in Japan for centuries. Although one type of sushi consists of a piece of raw fish placed on top of bite-sized pieces of rice, there are actually many different varieties. In addition to those featuring fish and shellfish, several other kinds of sushi are well suited to making in a classroom. The recipes that follow are for "inari-zushi" (fox sushi), "kappa-maki-zushi" (cucumber sushi), and "tamago sushi" (egg sushi). Soy sauce*—with or without *wasabi* (Japanese horseradish)**—is commonly used as dipping sauce, but optional here.

All sushi requires specially prepared rice. Make the rice ahead of time so it can cool before you start preparing the sushi. Students can be involved in the rice preparation as well.

Sushi Rice

About the Ingredients Japanese-style rice is grown in California and is widely available around the country, though it is fairly expensive. A good alternative is any medium grain rice. Though long grain rice will become hard after cooking, it will suffice if you plan to prepare and consume all the sushi in a short time. Rice vinegar has a milder taste than other kinds of vinegar. Using other types of vinegar will definitely alter the taste of your sushi rice.

DIRECTIONS

1. Pour the correct amount of rice into the pot in which you plan to cook it. A rice cooker is great, but if you don't have one, a heavier pot works best. Rinse rice thoroughly with cold water until the water runs clear. Then let it sit in the water for at least half an hour.

2. To use an electric rice cooker, follow the directions provided. To make rice on the stove, cover raw rice with water to about one inch above the top of the rice. Cover with a tight lid and bring to a boil. Uncover and boil until almost all of the water has been absorbed. Reduce heat to very low, cover, and cook until all water is absorbed. Turn off the heat but keep covered for about 15 minutes. Do not stir cooking rice.

3. Uncover the rice and add vinegar, sugar, and salt. Mix ingredients thoroughly into the cooked hot rice.

4. Allow the rice to cool to room temperature. Stir periodically.

MATERIALS

+ 2 cups Japanese-style or medium grain rice
+ 4 tablespoons rice vinegar
+ 3 tablespoons sugar
+ 2 teaspoons salt

* Do not use a sweet soy sauce. Most Asian groceries sell many brands of soy sauce.
**Wasabi* is a green-colored horseradish that has a strong taste. Many students don't care for it. You can buy *wasabi* either in cans of powder to be mixed with vinegar or water, or prepared in plastic tubes. A little goes a long way, so you won't need much.

Inari-zushi

Inari-zushi is fried bean curd stuffed with rice. Inari is the fox-deity; the sushi is called "inari" because the small packets of stuffed fried bean curd are reddish-brown in color and vaguely resemble fox tails. Although you have to buy the wrappers, this is the easiest form of sushi to make.

MATERIALS

+ You can buy *inari-zushi no moto* in many Asian grocery stores. There are about 17 little bean curd sacks in each can. These sacks are pre-seasoned and cooked. However, many people like to boil them again briefly and drain off the oily water.

DIRECTIONS

1. Open the inari-zushi no moto *carefully,* they open along one side, not at the ends.

2. Insert rice. Don't put in too much; you should be able to close up the opening with slight overlapping.

3. Arrange attractively on a plate, and eat!

Kappa-maki-zushi

This is often called "cucumber sushi" in Japanese restaurants in the United States. *Kappa* is a mythical Japanese creature whose favorite food is cucumber. Therefore, sushi rolled in seaweed wrapper (nori maki) with cucumber at its center is called *kappa-zushi*.

MATERIALS

+ sushi rolling mat

+ nori-type laver (seaweed) Choose packages of thin black sheets of laver. The number of sheets in each package varies greatly. Be sure to have one sheet for each student. The kind with perforated lines indicating where to slice is helpful.

+ cucumbers, sliced into long strips, lengthwise

DIRECTIONS

1. Wet the rolling mat and place it on a flat surface.

2. Spread one sheet of seaweed on top of the mat.

3. Working with wet hands, spread a layer of prepared rice on the lower third of the seaweed. The rice should no be more than about 1/4-inch thick.

4. Place slices of cucumber horizontally from one side of the seaweed to the other, in a line across the middle of the rice.

5. Wet the end of the seaweed that is farthest from the rice.

6. Now roll from the bottom, remembering to move the mat as you reach the top.

7. When it is completely rolled up, wrap the sushi in the mat and squeeze.

8. Push both ends in and remove the mat.

9. Slice the roll carefully along the perforated lines or in segments of about 3/4 of an inch.

Tamago Sushi

Although egg sushi does not need any unusual ingredients or equipment, it does require lots of cooking space.

DIRECTIONS

Ask students for assistance as you follow the instructions below:

1. Beat eggs in a large mixing bowl using a whisk, fork, or chopsticks.

2. Add salt and sugar to taste.

3. Heat a small amount of oil in the frying pan.

4. Pour enough of the egg mixture into the pan to coat the bottom.

5. As the egg begins to cook, use a fork or chopsticks and start rolling from one end. When the egg is completely rolled, remove from the pan and allow to cool.

6. With wet hands, make small patties of sushi rice. Each patty should fit in the hand.

7. When the rolled-up egg is cool, slice it into strips as wide as the rice patties.

8. Put a thin layer of wasabi on each patty (optional) and cover with a slice of egg.

MATERIALS

+ eggs
+ sugar
+ salt
+ mixing bowl
+ whisk, chopsticks, or fork
+ oil
+ frying pan
+ wasabi (Japanese horseradish)

FOLLOW-UP

I. *Discuss the origins of sushi. What are some of the advantages and disadvantages of this type of food?*

II. *Research the different kinds of sushi. What differences are there between the varieties of sushi common in Japan and those served in Japanese restaurants in the United States? Why might there be a difference?*

Field Trips

CHINA OR JAPAN

CONTEXT

There is no substitute for seeing something with your own eyes. Visiting a nearby art museum, experiencing a Chinese- or Japanese-style garden, or walking through a neighborhood of Asian stores and businesses will enhance your students' understanding and appreciation of the culture they are studying.

Encourage students to get some perspective of the entire exhibition or area, while focusing on particular works or features for further study. Using a trip sheet will help focus students so they can get the most out of their field trip. Try assigning every student the task of locating, observing, and recording what he or she sees. A good trip sheet has several characteristics, including:

- a design that ensures students observe carefully, not just glance at objects in passing.
- plenty of room for students to record, either with words or with illustrations, what they have seen.
- a flexible number of activities so that those students who work faster have enough to occupy their time productively, while those who work more slowly do not get frustrated or anxious.

Field trips can be something truly memorable for both you and your students. For that to happen, however, you need careful planning and preparation.

Before the Trip: Teacher Preparation

DIRECTIONS

1. Before you start creating the trip sheet, determine the goals of your excursion. Although this seems self-evident, it will help you to focus the activities you select for your students.

2. Visit the museum, garden, or neighborhood yourself first in order to compile the trip sheet. Locate and focus on those artifacts or features that you think are most representative, outstanding, or revealing. Plan your trip so the time you spend with students in a museum gallery or garden lasts about an hour to an hour and a half.

MATERIALS

✛ clipboards

✛ trip sheets

✛ pencils (not pens)

✛ colored pencils

✛ blank paper

If you are visiting a neighborhood, you might need more time.

3. Let the appropriate museum or garden personnel know that you're planning a class trip. Find out what their requirements are.

4. Find a way for students to get an overview of the exhibit, garden, or neighborhood. You can have them fill in a pre-drawn map, or ask them to locate and examine artifacts or features in different areas of the exhibit or garden. For example, in a museum, you might ask them to select and examine a landscape painting, a jade carving, a ceramic bowl, and a lacquer tray.

5. In a museum, focus students' attention primarily on the artifact itself, not on the information that accompanies it.

6. Look for ways to integrate other skills into the field trip experience. For example, mapping (geography skills) and poetry are useful curriculum connections.

Before the Trip: Class Preparation

Ideally, a field trip fits so perfectly into your curriculum that everything that has gone before is preparation and everything that comes after is follow-up. However, that is not always possible due to the exigencies of museum or transportation schedules. If the exhibit you are planning to visit is closing a month before you study the appropriate topic, consider rearranging your curriculum. If that's not practical, plan your trip as an opportunity for discovery, while still anchoring it to familiar material. Looking for comparisons is a good way to accomplish this. One way or the other, students must know where they are going and why, and what they can expect to see before they head out on a field trip.

Decide ahead of time if students will be allowed to make purchases. If you think it's all right, then be prepared. Make sure everyone knows that they don't have to buy something, and provide guidelines for parents and students alike as to how much money they should bring.

The Trip

1. Pass out trip sheets before you leave for your destination. Allow students at least a few minutes to glance over the material, and review any parts that require explanation.

2. Before you leave the classroom, be sure each student has a clipboard, trip sheet, pencil, transportation money (if necessary), and lunch (if necessary).

3. All museums, exhibits, and gardens have rules of behavior. Be sure your students understand the rules before you enter the building. If you are visiting a neighborhood or business area, discuss the appropriate ways to behave.

FOLLOW-UP

I. *When students return from their trip, they should be encouraged to think about their excursion while the experience is still fresh. For homework on the night of the outing, or in class the next day, have students go over their trip sheets carefully. They should correct, complete, or add to their written responses and drawings.*
II. *Have students describe their trip experiences in an essay or in poetry or story form.*

TEACHING TIPS

Try the activities yourself first, on location. Your students will require at least as much time as you do.

■

Bring along plenty of extra paper, pencils, and trip sheets. Clipboards are a must because most places you visit—including museums—lack hard surfaces where students can write or draw.

■

At a museum, make sure that the objects you have selected will be accessible to your students. For example, if an artifact is displayed at your eye level, it will probably be difficult for students to see clearly and easily.

■

While it is important for students to read some of the labels or captions included at a museum exhibit, they aren't really what your trip is about. You should visit a museum so your students can actually see the objects. Select displays and artifacts that are visually powerful and not overloaded with text.

■

If you are visiting a neighborhood or business area, talk to local merchants to advise them that you may be planning a trip to their place of business. Make sure your class will be welcome.

■

If you are venturing into a neighborhood or business area, make sure you have enough chaperones for your class.

■